Shattered

IN THE EYE
OF THE
STORM

FAYE D. RESNICK

WITH
JEANNE V. BELL

FOREWORD BY DOMINICK DUNNE

DOVE
B O O K S

This book is dedicated to my father in heaven, to Nicole and Ron, to those who walk the path with me, and to the goddess of strength in all women.

ISBN 0-7871-0730-1

Printed in the United States of America

Dove Books
301 North Cañon Drive
Beverly Hills, CA 90210

Distributed by Penguin USA

Text design by Bob Tinnon
Typesetting and layout by Michele Lanci-Altomare
Jacket design and layout by Rick Penn-Kraus
Jacket photograph by Anthony Nex

First Printing: February 1996
10 9 8 7 6 5 4 3 2 1

Contents

Acknowledgments

*T*his book took everything of me to write, and there were many people who helped me complete the task. I thank them all with love.

To my writing partner, Jeanne Viner Bell, who has been as loving as a mother, for giving her expertise, heart, and soul to me and to this book. To Tuffy, for his understanding. To Sally Nussbaum, for her work and dedication, and for never faltering.

To Warren Cowan, Michael Levine, and Wendy Walker, my publicists, for their professionalism and loving support.

To Rev. Dr. Michael Beckwith, for his spiritual guidance.

To Kelly Piper, my yoga teacher and psychic healer, for helping to center me through this madness.

To all of the creative and gentle staff at Dove Books.

To my loving sisters, Patricia and Victoria, who bring meaning to my life.

To my mother and father, for all their love. To my brothers, Curtis, Jeffrey, and Michael, for all their love and support.

To my ex-husband, Paul, and to my stepdaughters, Jennifer, Jessica, and Julie.

To my dear and loyal friends, Mary, CiCi, Kris, Candace, Robin, Kathy, Susie, Stacy, Melissa, Pearl, Penny, Jo Anne, James, Michael, David, Jerry, John, Rick, Larry, Steve, Enrico, and Bruce, for not only holding my hand through the toughest time in my life but also reminding me to breathe. You have been my guardian angels, and I love you all.

To my daughter, Francesca, for giving me the strength and courage to continue, and for reminding me what life is truly all about.

—Faye D. Resnick

WARM THANKS TO:

M.V. for believing in my ability.

Mary Aarons, for her interest and oversight.

Lee Montgomery, for caring and for her dedication to making this a better book.

Sally B. Nussbaum, for her input, her invaluable help and support, and her always wonderful sense of humor.

Erika Santos, for her willing assistance.

Kerry Stowell, for so generously sharing her knowledge and resources.

Ruth Brice, for her constructive insights.

Sabine Guibal, for her interest and advice.

Heidi Rosvold, editor of the Health Report of the National Women's Health Resource Center, for her gracious cooperation.

Gertrudes Francisco, for the care and feeding of authors.

Tuffy, who is planning to write a book on dog neglect.

—Jeanne Viner Bell

Foreword

*B*efore I saw Faye Resnick being interviewed by Connie Chung on "Eye to Eye," in anticipation of the publication of her book *Nicole Brown Simpson: The Private Diary of a Life Interrupted*, I was disinclined to believe her. I remember that I said things like, "How could she?" without having read a word of her book, as if she were a betrayer. I had an advance copy, but I had treated it as an artifact rather than something to read, a camp object for a coffee table at my house in Connecticut. Watching Resnick that night with Chung, she came off as being a completely different person than I had pegged her as being. I learned very quickly that this was no airhead cashing in on her friend's murder. She didn't mince her words. She said exactly what she thought. She was smart. She knew the score. To my amazement, words like *brave* and *fearless* came to my mind.

Then I read her book. Sure it was dirty. Sure I could have done without the blow-job episode, where the guy wakes up from his sleep and says "Thanks" to Nicole. But the book had a sense of truth to it, even honor, in a Brentwood sort of way. I was mesmerized. She portrayed expertly the telling moments of control, belittlement, and cruelty in the post-marital relationship of Nicole and O.J. Simpson. Previously, they had been the victim and the defendant to me, Nicole lying in a pool of blood in a short black dress and O.J. sitting at the defense table looking cool, calm, and collected. Resnick turned them into people. She visualized their lives and brought into focus the actions and the reasons that led up the terrible events of June 12, 1994. I believed her.

I said to Michael Viner one day early in the trial, "I'd like to meet Faye Resnick." He arranged it. We had dinner one night in a Beverly Hills apartment with two of Nicole's other friends, CiCi Shahian and Robin Greer. I have always heard that you can tell the worth of a woman by the way her female friends feel about her. Those three loved Nicole, wanted me to know what Nicole was like, and wanted her killer to be brought to justice. "Nicole always said, 'He's going to kill me and get away with it,'" said Faye that night. I remarked during the evening that there were people who did not believe Simpson was guilty, as we all did. She tossed back her hair impatiently and said, "The kind of people who think O.J. didn't do it are not the kind of people he wants to be with." That line told it like it turned out to be.

Like a lot of people connected with the Simpson saga, Faye became famous after the enormous success of her book. People stared at her in restaurants. She was always on television, sounding off, looking beautiful. Once I saw her walk into Drai's restaurant, at the peak hour when the restaurant was mobbed, and she reminded me of Gene Tierney in *The Razor's Edge* as she crossed the room, every eye on her. But, unlike a few people I could mention, and will mention in my own book on this extraordinary event that we both played a part in, Faye didn't change with her celebrity, never veered from her firm belief, always talked truth. Johnnie Cochran never missed a chance to announce to Judge Ito and the world at large that the trial was a "search for truth, Your Honor," while telling us at the same time that O.J. was chipping golf balls at ten o'clock at night at the estate on Rockingham while some Colombian drug dealers were over at the condo on Bundy slashing the throats of Nicole and Ron Goldman because they thought Nicole was Faye Resnick, who owed them money for an unpaid drug bill.

Yeah, sure, Johnnie. Truth was a joke at the trial. Truth became what they got the jury to believe. Once, after the verdict, when we were reeling from the shock of Simpson's acquittal, Faye and I were both on Larry King at the same time. I could tell she had been crying, but she pulled it together like the pro she had become, went on, and ridiculed the outcome. Before the American backlash to the verdict, she was at the forefront of condemning it.

—Dominick Dunne
Los Angeles, California

Introduction

*I*t is perhaps interesting that as I began to write this introduction, we were in the final days of the O.J. Simpson double-murder trial. It was a cool, cloudy Tuesday, September 26, 1995, exactly one year since the selection of the jury, fifteen months since Nicole Brown Simpson and Ron Goldman were murdered, and a little under a year since the publication of my book *The Private Diary of a Life Interrupted.*

That morning Marcia Clark began the prosecution's closing arguments. Later that evening Christopher Darden delivered a compelling, eloquent closing that made viewers around the world shiver. As he spoke about the murders, detailing the act and the accused killer's premeditation, anger, and rage, Nicole's mother and sister, Juditha and Tanya, sobbed. "And he stabs and he cuts and he slices until that rage is gone . . . and the rage that he has . . . it flows out of him . . . and into the knife and from the knife into her. . . ."

Less than a week later the trial of the century was over and O.J. Simpson was a free man. Now, months later, network satellite crews have moved on to distant cities and other sensational news and tabloids have moved on to other prey. Over time the tragedy will fade into silence. The world will go on. We will continue to live our lives, but none of us will ever be the same. The trial of former American football hero O.J. Simpson for the brutal murders of Nicole Brown Simpson and Ronald Goldman has changed our lives. The publicity. The cruelty. The cameras. The factions. The lies. The horror.

One of my main objectives for writing *Private Diary* was to document what I knew to be the truth behind the murders of Nicole Brown Simpson and Ron Goldman. It was my greatest hope that the people who read about Nicole Brown and O.J. Simpson's tragic relationship would be able to gain greater insight into one of our nation's biggest tragedies: domestic violence. In the best of worlds I wanted to empower people to leave abusive relationships and at the very least to have them gain a better understanding of the problem and seek help.

Although I had high hopes surrounding the publication of *Private Diary*, I had no idea about what was in store for me. Looking back over the last year, I see it has been a tumultuous, painful time at best; one that has exceeded not only my dreams for the project, but also my worst nightmares. The good news is people were reaching out; the bad news is they were reaching out in record numbers. The good news is, by stepping forward and speaking out, some people's lives have changed for the better; the bad news is, when it comes to public figures and celebrity trials, terms like "honesty" and "justice" seem to be distant reminders of a time gone by.

In the foreword of *Private Diary* I wrote, ". . . if this book inspires even one woman to seek help in escaping the cycle of violence . . . then any embarrassment I suffer will be an acceptable price to pay." I now know the book has been successful in its goal and for that I am extremely grateful, but I also know that this success has come at quite a price.

On June 12, 1994, two innocent people were brutally and senselessly murdered. One of them was my dearest friend. At that moment every aspect of my life was shattered irrevocably and forever. Nicole Brown Simpson knew she was going to die, and because I was compelled to tell this truth, because I felt this information had to be known, I became the target of O.J. Simpson and his friends and lawyers, as well as the media.

What you are about to read is the story behind the headlines. The names, characters, places, and incidents are *not* the product of my imagination or used fictitiously. Any resemblance to actual events or locales or persons, living or dead, is *not* coincidental. And in the end, when all is said and done and you close this book, you are free to call me what you like. Call me a rebel. Call me a profiteer, but realize this: Domestic violence is not a figment of my imagination, and believe me when I tell you there is a very high price to pay for speaking the truth.

—Faye D. Resnick
October 1995

Where language and naming are power, silence is oppression, is violence.

—Adrienne Rich

PART I

Shattered

Girl, you—out of all of them—
know that I loved her too much.

—O.J. Simpson to Faye Resnick
at Nicole's funeral

Chapter 1

EXODUS

I was three days into a treatment program at
Exodus Recovery Center in Marina del Rey when
Nicole was murdered. It had happened exactly as
she said it would, and after I learned of her death, I
quickly realized the knowledge I had about her life
with O.J.—the arguments, the threats, the
humiliation, the beatings—could put my life in
danger. I was terrified that I was next. When I
explained this to the Exodus counselors, they
assured me that Exodus's security was excellent and
I had no cause to worry as long as I was there.

Even knowing that I was safe as long as I stayed
in the hospital, I could not sleep. I kept thinking
somebody was going to come in the middle of the

night and slit my throat the same way the killer had slit Nicole's. The image came back to me over and over. I knew O.J. was still walking the streets. I knew that his boyhood buddy, the ever-faithful A.C. Cowlings, would do anything O.J. wanted done, anytime. I kept wondering how I would be murdered. Who would do it? Would it be O.J. or one of his pals, or would he hire someone to do the job for him?

I knew they couldn't get to me at Exodus, but I felt it was just a matter of time. On several occasions O.J. had told me he would kill Nicole. I couldn't determine where his threats came from or whether or not they were true, but I knew I couldn't dismiss them. I knew about his fits of rage and his cruelty. I knew he had hurt Nicole in the past. She had told me and other friends that she expected O.J. would kill her.

These were the thoughts racing through my mind during the first several days after the murders. Life had become so strange I began to think that it would be better to die than to go through even one more day of not knowing what terrible blow was going to strike me next.

Nicole was murdered on Sunday. I was told about it on Monday. The viewing of Nicole's body was planned for Wednesday afternoon at a funeral home in Laguna Beach, and the funeral was scheduled for the following Thursday morning at St. Martin of Tours Church in Brentwood.

Although I wanted very much to go to the viewing, I was too devastated to attend. I had been crying nonstop and couldn't bear the thought of seeing Nicole like that. Though our "friend," Cora Fishman, told the press I was too busy having my hair done, the truth was I didn't have the strength to leave the hospital.

On Thursday morning Christian Reichardt, my then-fiancé, a chiropractor I had been seeing on and off for four years who was also a friend of O.J. and Nicole's, picked me up at Exodus and took me to St. Martin's for the funeral service. On the way there I struggled to tell Christian what was happening to me. I told him I was frightened that I would be murdered and it was a feeling so deep, so horrifying, I couldn't shake it.

He turned and looked at me as if I had completely lost my mind. "You're just being melodramatic," he said.

* * *

The funeral was madness. O.J. was deep, dark, and gloomy, but still trying to be the star of the show.

He was heavily sedated and it was obvious that he had been told not to talk to anybody. But O.J., being O.J., couldn't restrain himself from trying to find out which friends would be his advocates and which would be his opponents. And he was carrying on as if *he* were the victim, not Nicole. That was his new act and he stayed with it.

During the funeral, as I walked up to the altar to receive my blessing, I heard Nicole's son, Justin, call my name. I turned and walked toward him and Sydney, who were standing behind me. Suddenly O.J. was in my path. He grabbed my hand and spoke in a raspy, strained voice. "Girl, I want to talk to you."

"O.J., this is about Nicole," I said. "This is not about you and it is not the time to have any discussions."

As we left the church, there were cameras everywhere and helicopters circling over our heads, which followed us on our ninety-minute drive to the cemetery in Laguna Beach. It seemed a cruel end for Nicole.

At Nicole's grave her mother, Juditha, read aloud the words, "If anyone knows of this, please tell me now!" My first thought was, *She knows exactly what happened. Why is she asking anyone else?* Juditha had been one of O.J.'s closest confidantes, so she knew all there was to know.

My next thought was, *Stand up and speak out! Say that O.J. told me he would kill Nicole.* Then I realized that this was a time for peace, not accusations. Still, it was nearly impossible to keep silent when I knew O.J. was walking around as a free man while Nicole was gone forever. After the service I looked at some of Nicole's favorite pictures on top of the casket. I was looking at the photo of a group of us in Cabo San Lucas taken only a month and a half before. There was Christian, Nicole, O.J., me and others.

"We were so happy," I heard O.J. say from behind me.

I turned to him and asked, "What happened, O.J., what happened?"

"Girl, you—out of all of them—know that I loved her too much."

He was right. I knew he had loved her too much. I also knew that he had wanted to kill her, as he had once told me on the telephone, because she was "affecting his image" and he was not going to let her get away with it. She had divorced him, gone back to him, and then left him again. Apparently it was more than he could handle.

Throughout the trial, every time I saw him sitting serenely in the courtroom surrounded by his lawyers like a king among his courtiers, I heard the same three phrases in my head over and over:

O.J. saying, "I'll kill her, I swear I will."

Then at the cemetery: "Girl, you—out of all of them—know that I loved her too much."

And Nicole saying, "He's going to kill me and make it look as if it's my fault. And he's going to get away with it!"

We've all heard the cliché "getting away with murder." It now has a new and terrible meaning for me.

* * *

I returned to Exodus right after the funeral. Losing Nicole was horrible enough, but the fact that she had been killed so brutally made it even worse. Images of her played over and over again in my mind. I knew I needed time to grieve and felt I needed to begin that process while still at Exodus, where I had a good support system around me.

I guess I was lucky to be in treatment at the time of the murders. If I had not been, there's no question that I would have been with Nicole on the night of Sydney's dance recital. And if I had heard anything, of course I would have run out to help. I shudder to think about what could have happened. I kept thinking, *If I had just been there, maybe I could have done something.* . . . The counselors kept saying, "You should thank God that you weren't there, because there is nothing you could have done to change what happened."

I couldn't believe that Nicole was really dead, and everything seemed to be getting more bizarre by the moment. That first week was like watching a nightmare unfold. It was the week of the car chase and the funeral and the ridiculous rumors about my alleged drug connections and Colombian cartels.

On the day of the infamous low-speed car chase I was still at Exodus in a group meeting, and through the windows I could see the helicopters that were following O.J.'s white Ford Bronco. The person next to me had a radio with earphones and was telling us about the people cheering O.J. on. The meeting came to a halt so that we—and, I've heard, at least half of America—could follow the chase.

It was a bizarre scene. There was a stream of police cars following the Bronco, and there were mobs of people lining the freeway and crowded onto every overpass holding signs that said things like Go, Juice, you're the best. I was over-whelmed hearing this adulation for a man who had just murdered his wife!

I thought back to the day before, the last time I'd seen him and A.C. It was at the Browns' home after Nicole's burial. A few of us were talking in the courtyard. There had been a phone call and then a rumor that there was a warrant for O.J.'s arrest. I had watched through the window as, inside, O.J. and Al Cowlings got up and went into the master bedroom, closing the door behind them.

Nicole's and my friend, Kris Jenner, said, "Look at that. O.J. and A.C. are going to pull the same stunt they've been pulling for the past twenty years. Whenever O.J.'s in trouble, A.C. is there to cover for him. Now they're going to change clothes. That's what they do when O.J. wants to get away from somewhere unnnoticed."

Moments later O.J. walked out—and then I realized that it wasn't O.J. at all, but A.C. in O.J.'s clothes. He walked out of the house with O.J.'s security guards, and the helicopters whirling overhead followed him as they drove away. Meanwhile O.J., disguised in A.C.'s clothes, slipped away unseen.

Remembering that scene so vividly as I sat and listened to the low-speed chase was a chilling moment and a tragic punctuation to my friend's murder. The situation seemed to grow more surreal by the minute. When it was reported that O.J. said he was going to see his mother for the last time, I thought, *Sure he is—his mother lives in San Francisco,*

*which is north, and he's going south toward the border.
Are these people really believing this man?*

He was behaving like a caged animal. He went
from saying, "Who, me?" to being so frightened he
jumped into his Bronco with his boyhood friend
and drove away with a beard, a mustache, a gun,
his passport, and $10,000 in cash. Couldn't people
see these weren't the actions of an innocent man?
They were so overwhelmed with sympathy for
"poor O.J. Simpson, it was as if nobody really
understood what he was doing."

Even though he had traveled well beyond the
cemetery, he said he was going to visit Nicole's
grave. Then why didn't he? When he tried to
arouse public sympathy by saying he was going to
commit suicide, my initial thought was: *Please, O.J.,
do it! Do not drag your family and friends down with
you. Take responsibility for your actions and get it over
with, especially for Sydney and Justin's sake.*

When A.C. told the police to back off because
O.J. was about to shoot himself, I knew he didn't
have the capacity to kill himself. He was running. It
was rumored through friends that he was headed
for a private plane at the Ontario Airport, but
District Attorney Gil Garcetti appeared on a special
broadcast and warned that anyone helping O.J.
escape would be charged with aiding and abetting a

fugitive. So that plan was out. And O.J. knew full well he could never cross the border into Mexico without being arrested. He was too well known and the border patrol had been put on alert.

When O.J. called his mother on the cellular phone in the Bronco, it was intercepted and recorded by the police. According to several newspapers, during the conversation O.J.'s mother told him to plead insanity and give himself up. O.J. said it wasn't his fault; his and Nicole's marriage had been doomed from the beginning.

As he neared Brentwood, O.J. apparently called Nicole's home on Bundy knowing the Browns were there. When he told them he was on his way, they became extremely nervous and called the police. O.J. was running out of places to run to. Every door was closing in his face one by one.

Soon the helicopters were over Brentwood, and O.J. and A.C. finally drove up to the house at Rockingham. The news crews surrounded the estate, and O.J.'s son Jason came running out. Some people believe that Jason stopped his father from committing suicide, but I believe O.J. had no intention of committing suicide because he always said he was above the law. Suicide was just a ploy to arouse public support—and it worked beautifully.

To add to the confusion of the chase, Robert Kardashian appeared on TV and read O.J.'s suicide note, which was written expressly to get the world on O.J.'s side. When Robert read off the names of all O.J.'s buddies, it made me ill. He was asking them to cover up for O.J. Then he went on to say that all of Nicole's girlfriends would confirm that O.J. had done everything in his power to keep the marriage together. O.J. was asking us to protect him!

I was furious. How dare the man who had butchered Nicole ask us to lie and cover up for him? Kris Jenner, CiCi Shahian, Robin Greer, Candace Garvey, and I were totally amazed by his audacity.

Nothing surprised me about that letter except the fact that O.J., who sat on the boards of so many corporations, could not even spell the simplest words. And most interesting, but just as tragic, there was not a word of sympathy for the woman he supposedly loved, the mother of his children. All I heard was a plea for all his friends to remember that he was a lost soul and to feel sorry for him and protect him. I think that if he had been innocent, what he would have said was, "Please find out who did this awful crime and protect my family."

* * *

A couple of days after Nicole's funeral, after O.J. was arrested, Christian visited me at Exodus and told me about the rumors he had been hearing. "There's a story going around that someone who was trying to collect money from a drug deal was really after you and killed Nicole instead. Also, they're saying that you and Nicole were involved with a drug ring."

I was stunned. I couldn't believe that anyone could create such a dreadful, deceitful rumor.

* * *

When I left Exodus about two weeks later, I was so nervous about what O.J. or O.J.'s people might do to me that I went straight to the office of my attorney, Arthur Barens. I explained, "I know information that would incriminate O.J. and I feel that I could be killed because of it. I need you to document it. If I am murdered, I want people to know who killed the three of us."

After listening to some of the details, Arthur said, "This has to be told and I think it should be in a book. If you give this information to the prosecution, they will have to turn it over to the defense team immediately, and then you really will be seen as a threat. Your safest bet is to get it to the public."

Later that evening I told Christian that Arthur thought I should write a book and I was considering doing it. I also told him that I was too nervous to stay alone and said, "I think it would be good for me to start working at your office again and get my mind on something besides what happened to Nicole. I can't stop thinking about it and it's making me crazy."

Christian then informed me that I no longer had my job managing his practice. I was puzzled. "Why is that?" He said that people from the media might come looking for me to talk about Nicole, and he didn't want them around his office.

I felt as if he was deliberately trying to crush me. "So, once again you are more interested in your office than you are in my well-being."

He sort of mumbled, "You shouldn't think of it that way."

My answer was, "Christian, that's the only way to think of it."

A few days later Kris and Bruce Jenner, Candace and Steve Garvey, and Christian and I went to Toscana for my birthday. We had just started dinner when one of O.J.'s lead lawyers,

Robert Shapiro, came in with his wife and son. They were seated right next to us, and our table immediately fell silent. We ate quickly, without speaking. I knew then that not only was everything falling apart in my life, but I also could no longer expect to have any real peace and privacy again.

Chapter 2

READING FUTURES

*D*uring the weeks following Nicole's murder, I was overwhelmed by the feeling she was near me. Every time I drove around a corner, I would see something that reminded me of her. Or I would pick up the phone to call her without even thinking. I just couldn't find a way to get over it. Every day seemed to bring something else that would tear at me. It was all too much. I felt that my life was shattered—I could see only misery and pain in my future. I was even becoming convinced that I no longer had anything positive to offer my daughter, Francesca, and that after the defense team was finished with their attacks on my her father, Paul Resnick. I knew that Paul loved her and would give her the care, guidance, attention, and stability she should have.

It hadn't taken O.J.'s lawyers very long to turn the impending trial into a circus, and I felt like I was the tiger in their cage. I didn't want to put my daughter through that, and I didn't know if I had the strength to go through it, either. The bad press had already started, and the media had begun its ugly descent.

Francesca and I were back at Christian's because I desperately needed the emotional support, and despite my problems with Christian, I didn't have the strength to leave him yet. I knew I needed some time to collect myself, but the situation was already well out of control. I was receiving telephone messages from O.J. in jail—I think about five or six in total—and calls from reporters by the dozens. I couldn't deal with what was happening. I remember feeling captive in Christian's condominium. There were so many media people calling and coming to my door at all hours, and I didn't want to have anything to do with them.

Minutes after I returned from Exodus, one journalist was already on the phone. "This is Tony Frost," he said into my machine. "I'm from the

Star and I just want you to know that I know where you've been. I also know that you were one of Nicole's best friends and I need to talk to you."

I ignored the call, of course. I did not want to talk to any member of the media, especially one from a tabloid. I stopped answering my phone and started screening the calls because they were coming in around the clock. I don't know how these people got my number, but they did and I must have been high on their list of people to bother.

Tony Frost's calls kept coming, usually about four times a day. He'd leave messages on my answering machine—"I know you're there and I just want you to verify [this or that], so call me back as soon as you can." I began to feel like he lived outside my front door.

One day I heard Frost leaving a message on my machine about a story the *Star* was planning to publish about Kato Kaelin and Nicole being lovers. According to Frost, somebody had seen them together in Aspen, and he knew that I was very well aware of it. As I listened to him rattle on, I became furious. Finally, a few days later when he called, I picked up the phone and said, "I don't know where you're getting your information, but it is not accurate. Nicole never had an affair with

Kato. It definitely is not true."

At the time Tony reminded me that he knew about me being in rehab and he had never exposed that.

"I know you're one of the good guys," he said. "I also know that you've been victimized. I've been hearing all the rumors that the defense team is floating and I want to be on your side. But I can't be unless I have the facts. I know Nicole was murdered and I don't want to murder her again. But if I'm getting misinformation then I need her friends to tell what's true and what's not. So, if you could just corroborate a few things it would be very helpful."

I thought, *Well, if he wants some information, I'll tell him about the person who is trying to slander Nicole and trying to slander me.* So I agreed to meet with him, planning to tell him what I had been hearing about one of the lead lawyers on O.J.'s defense team. Although he was married, he was rumored to be having an affair with a pretty young blonde. The alleged mistress shared her home with a good friend of mine who knew "Mr. X" was visiting at odd hours and leaving at two-thirty in the morning. I thought to myself, *This man is doing everything he can to make Nicole look bad. People should know that he has some skeletons in his own closet.*

So I said, "Okay, Tony, if you want to see me, I'll meet with you."

It's amazing how quickly Tony Frost was able to get information from so many of Nicole's friends and so-called friends. He threw money at them left and right, trying to get them to speak with him. I told him that if I did pass on information to him, I wanted him to send the money to Nicole's children. He said that would be fine, so I agreed to meet with him.

We met at Le Dôme restaurant one evening. Our meeting lasted for about thirty minutes. I never mentioned anything about the defense lawyer because Tony made it clear that he was interested in primarily the personal lives of O.J. and Nicole. After I left him, I felt he was concerned only with his magazine's circulation and had no interest in helping Nicole. I resolved not to have anything more to do with him.

Later, when Christian heard that I had met with Tony Frost, he became infuriated, pounding holes in the walls and throwing perfume bottles at me. He did not want me giving any information to the press; he was thinking about Arthur Barens's suggestion for a book, which he wanted to co-author with me.

* * *

This marked the beginning of what I call the Era of Misinformation. Although the lies surrounding the case still continue, and probably will long after the verdict, they were completely out of control in the early days. People I had never seen or heard of were appearing on TV saying they had known Nicole well. There were also countless stories flying around in the press that I knew were not true. It was madness of the highest order.

It was during this time at the end of June that Jerry Ginsberg, an old friend of Nicole's and mine, called me from out of the blue. Although he lives in New York, he was in Los Angeles on business. I think he could sense how upset I was because one of the first things he mentioned was that he had just returned from seeing his psychic, Elizabeth Ridgewood, and he thought she might be able to provide me with some much-needed perspective and comfort.

Jerry had spoken of her before. In fact, Nicole and I had already made and canceled an appointment to see her about a year before. I was so desperate for the comfort Jerry said I might find with her, and wanted so much to do something that Nicole and I had once planned to do together, that I made an appointment to see Elizabeth the next day.

I did not know anything about this woman, only that Jerry thought highly of her. At our first meeting I did not reveal anything about myself. I just wanted to hear what she had to say. Elizabeth began by telling me that I had a guide who was trying to help me. Then she looked at me and exclaimed, "I feel an amazing force of power around you. Someone who has recently passed on wants to communicate with you."

She continued by telling me that a woman who loved me and missed me very much wanted to give me a message. I felt myself trembling when I thought of Nicole. Elizabeth told me that the woman was encouraging me to move forward, trust my instincts, and continue to tell the truth.

At that point I told Elizabeth that my attorney had advised me to write a book. She nodded and said, "That's what you are being called to do, and from your friend's message, I know that's where your journey will take you."

I protested that I did not have the ability or stamina to follow through. Elizabeth assured me that I did, and said that I should try to avoid making any judgments—I should just write what I knew.

When I replied that if I was to write what I knew, I would not be able to avoid making judgments, she whispered, "I fear for you." Then, the last thing she said was, "You will write that book. That's what you are supposed to do."

All the way home I kept thinking, *I cannot write a book. It's all too much for me.* And by the time I walked in the door, I knew that I did not have the strength to continue. The last few weeks had been so difficult, I didn't feel like I could go on. The meeting with Tony Frost had convinced me that it wouldn't be long before the media would know that I had been in drug treatment. And I still felt that it was only a matter of time until I would be murdered. It seemed gentler and easier to overdose on pills than wait for someone to come and kill me. And I thought that if I took my own life, the endless rumors would stop. The media would be forced to focus on my death instead of smearing my reputation and hurting my child. So I took Francesca to her father's house, kissed my beautiful daughter one last time, and told her how much I loved her.

When I got back to Christian's, I took the bottle of Valium from the bathroom closet where I had been hiding it, opened it, and poured a glass of water. And at that moment, standing there in the bathroom readying myself to swallow the pills, I became overwhelmed with the memory of Nicole. She seemed nearby, at least in my thoughts and my heart. I was so saddened by her death and by what happened during the months leading up to it. I wanted so much to have been able to help her end her feelings of helplessness, to have been able to help her move forward in her life and away from her relationship with O.J. Yet I was not able to stop her murder. At that moment I realized I had to make a contribution in her memory. I had to tell the truth. I had to tell her story. I put down the pills and realized then that if I could find the strength and the courage to explain what had happened to her through all those years, that this would be the greatest gift of all, not only for Nicole, but for the others who were suffering like she had.

Those moments spent thinking about Nicole gave me the strength to face the overwhelming task that lay ahead. Now, looking back a year later, I wonder: *If I had known then what was in my future, would I have made the same decision? Would I have been able to carry on?* Believe me, throughout this period, the most difficult ever in my life, I have thought about committing suicide many times, but two people have kept me going: Nicole and my daughter, Francesca. I could not bear the thought of letting either of them down.

* * *

That evening when Christian came home, I told him I had made a decision. I had decided to write the book.

Christian said, "Okay, fine, you are going to write a book. But whatever you do, don't go to the prosecution and don't talk to anybody about what you know."

"Why shouldn't I go to the prosecution and tell them my plans?" I asked. "I want them to know what I am doing."

Christian repeated, "I do not want you going to the prosecution." Then he insisted again that I was never to tell anyone about O.J.'s death threats to Nicole. He implied that he was trying to protect me. At first I believed him—that was my delusion about his love for me. It took me a while to realize that it had nothing to do with me—he was trying to protect O.J.

A day or two later Christian announced that he had decided to do the book with me and he wanted part of any money that would come from it. I did not care if he took it all—that was the last thing on my mind. When I told him that the major point of the book was to shed some light on domestic violence, he had the nerve to look me in the eye and say, "That has nothing to do with this case."

I could only answer, "Christian, it is all about domestic violence. Nicole was beaten throughout her life with O.J. and she was murdered because he could not control her. It has to be told so that other women can save themselves."

Christian was upset when he heard that. He also was furious when he learned that I had already gone to the prosecution's office. "I want nothing more to do with this," he said, clenching his teeth. When he understood that I was determined to write about the abuse and that I had told the truth to the prosecution, he accused me of betraying him. He, like O.J., was now the victim.

We got into another raging fight and I finally said, "I have been deluded. You are not the person I thought you were and you and I are finished. I will write this book and it will have nothing to do with you. This book will be about Nicole, about O.J., and about domestic violence."

That night I packed Francesca's and my bags and left. I went to stay with Kris and Bruce Jenner, where I knew I would be safe because O.J.'s lawyer and friend Robert Kardashian had his children living with Kris, their mother.

The following day I made arrangements to have Francesca stay with her father while I was gone. Four days later I was in Vermont and had begun work on the book about Nicole.

Chapter 3

LIFE WITH CHRISTIAN

I had been seeing Christian Reichardt for two years before I introduced him to Nicole and O.J. Like many people who met O.J., it didn't take long for Christian to fall under O.J.'s spell. Christian considered O.J. a demigod but his loyalty was also motivated by money. He was impressed by O.J.'s fame, power, and wealth. Nicole and O.J. were having problems in their relationship and Christian never understood why Nicole wanted to leave. When I tried to explain that O.J. had beaten her before and she was certain it would happen again, Christian did not consider that a valid reason. His view was that O.J. gave Nicole a life of luxury, so she should just go along with whatever he wanted and, it seemed, put up with whatever he did to her.

It was not long until Christian had financial ties to O.J. Soon after I introduced them, Christian, who specialized in sports medicine, thought that aligning himself with famous athletes would help build his chiropractic practice—if my friends O.J., Steve Garvey, and Bruce Jenner would recommend him to others, then he'd be set. He started treating O.J. whenever O.J. had an ache or a pain and, of course, Christian never let him pay for his treatments.

Not only did Christian find O.J. very useful in his business, but he was flattered to be seen with a superstar. When you were with O.J. Simpson, everybody around would look at you as if you must be someone interesting or important. And Christian was very impressed. As far as I'm concerned, being out with O.J. was quite frankly a pain in the ass. The only reason I was around him was because, even though she was increasingly unhappy with him, Nicole insisted on having O.J. in her life.

Christian liked being a part of O.J.'s circle—he liked the dinners and the vacations. But he was also very much aware of the financial potential for his own career. Christian's agenda with O.J.

became increasingly clear to me, and it was one of the reasons I knew I would leave him someday.

Right before the murders, when O.J. started sensing that Nicole really was reaching the end with him, he'd help her friends in order to win their loyalty. One day he asked Christian, "I have a project that might interest you. Would you like to go into business with me?"

Christian said, "Of course I would!" The deal was that Playboy wanted O.J. to do some videos on what he did to get over jet lag when he traveled. I heard Christian ask him, "Well, what do you do?"

"I do the same thing as everybody else—I just sleep it off. But I can't sell that," O.J. said, "so I need you to write out for me what I can say I do before I travel, during the flight, and after I get where I'm going. Everything I do to stay fit."

Christian jumped right in. "This is what you do. . . ." and went on to describe a complete plan—the group of vitamins and supplements O.J. would need and his eating plan before, during, and after trips. He told O.J. to explain that he starts taking the vitamins before he travels, that he carries Evian water and drinks at least a quart during the flight, that he continues taking the vitamins after the flight, and that as soon as he lands he goes immediately to the hotel and exercises.

O.J. said, "I certainly do not exercise in my hotel room. But I guess it's important to say I do, and we can show me going through some routine."

Actually, O.J. never did follow any part of what Christian prescribed, but Playboy was going to distribute 100,000 videos and Christian was supposed to get something like 10 percent of whatever O.J. made on the deal. Of course, Christian was more than delighted to be a part of it.

Another facet of the project was that O.J. would invest the money for Christian to develop and manufacture some exercise equipment that O.J. could demonstrate, saying that he used it on all his trips. Christian asked me to help him with some research and I went to many different sources to see what was on the market and how we could modify the design to suit our purposes. I found a manufacturer—Earl Trusty at Farrufino's in Culver City—who could make what we wanted. Christian met with Earl and explained that if the Playboy venture worked out as he hoped, he would be ordering 100,000 units that would be paid for by O.J.

In the meantime, Christian wrote a four- or five-page article for O.J. and many pages of detailed directions on how frequent travelers can stay in shape.

When I told Nicole about their deal, she said, "Please tell Christian not to get involved with O.J. It spells trouble. He gets every single person who is close to me financially involved with him, and there's always a catch to it—usually some legal problem that O.J. can hold over them and say, 'You were involved in this with me.'"

Later, Nicole pleaded with Christian, "Please stay away from it—you don't know what you're getting into. This man is using you. Please, Christian, don't be a business partner with him."

His response was, "We've already started."

Christian's relationship with O.J. was based on the friendship of four people—two couples—Faye and Christian, and Nicole and O.J. So that was another reason Christian felt that Nicole should stay in the marriage—he needed her to maintain his ties to O.J.

* * *

As close as Nicole and I were, it wasn't until after her now-famous 911 call that she finally told me about the years of vicious beatings. It was then that I told Christian that I would rather not be around O.J. I couldn't stand his mistreatment of Nicole or his dramatic moods. Every time we would go anywhere, I was aware that at any moment O.J. might decide to pick a fight with Nicole or make a big scene about absolutely nothing. If Nicole said the wrong word or if a man happened to look at her in a way that bothered O.J., his eyes would glaze over, then he would break into a sweat, grab Nicole, and half drag her to his car. It was painful to see Nicole looking so frightened and humiliated.

Soon after they decided to reconcile, O.J. seemed to be getting stranger every week. Right after our last trip to Mexico, less than three months before the murders, O.J. told Christian and the other men in our group that it was up to them to "control their women." Whether it was telling us we couldn't smoke or his sudden decision that Nicole was not to go anywhere unless she was with him, he was doing everything he could to keep her more and more isolated.

Although O.J. flared up many times when both Christian and I were around, Christian would never admit to seeing the crazed side of O.J. In fact, Christian never seemed to see anything wrong with anything O.J. might do.

It's difficult to explain Christian's behavior. When I first met him, he seemed gentle, loving, and sensitive but after some time he started to show his temper. After he met O.J., he became worse than ever. He seemed to take on O.J.'s personality. O.J. always blamed Nicole for whatever problem he might be having, and suddenly anything that went wrong for Christian was my fault. For the six months before Nicole's death, Christian was O.J.'s disciple.

This later became the period of time that, during the trial, O.J.'s lawyer Johnnie Cochran alleged that I was begging Christian for dollars and drugs, which was ridiculous—Christian was the one who had terminal problems with money. Also according to Johnnie Cochran, Christian tried to talk me out of having breast-implant surgery because he felt that the pain and emotional stress would drive me to drugs. Every once in a while Cochran is half right. Though it is true that Christian did not want me to have the breast implants, it wasn't because he was concerned that I would use drugs. It was because he felt he might lose me. Even though it was at O.J.'s insistence that Nicole had her breasts enlarged, O.J. would often say, "As soon as the titty fairy comes around, you lose your woman."

Contrary to Cochran's allegations, Christian never remotely suggested that it would be bad for my health or drive me to drugs. Nevertheless, Christian hated every minute of it. He hated me for going against his wishes and he kept insisting that I wanted the operation because I was planning to leave him. I had left him before and even though I had always come back, he never felt sure I would stay.

In a sense he was right—not about why I had breast implants, but about my thoughts of leaving him. In retrospect, I can see that both Nicole and I stayed with men who abused or took advantage of us. Now that I understand more about battered woman syndrome, I realize that we were following the classic pattern that has kept millions of women trapped in abusive relationships.

After the operation, Christian was more convinced than ever that I'd leave him, and he became increasingly aggressive. From the moment I came home from the hospital, whenever I said anything that did not strike him just right, he would start throwing things. His anger was getting more intense. He was no longer anything like the man I had fallen in love with.

For some strange reason, Christian's usual time to attack me was when I was in the bathtub. He would start yelling and throw my perfume bottles or anything else he could get his hands on. There were holes in the wall and deep dents all over the door from his tirades.

Then, during one of his tantrums—about a week before Nicole's murder—he barely missed hitting me with a bottle, and that was it. I said, "I'm leaving. I now know that you would actually injure me. This is not what I want in my life. I cannot stay with a man who would harm me."

I have often asked myself why I allowed it to go that far. I guess I thought once Christian vented his rage, he'd get over it, but after the last bathtub episode I realized he had a serious problem. I broke our engagement and told Christian that our relationship was over. I said, "You need to leave here until I find a home for Francesca and me. I'm not willing to live with you any longer. I am not about to subject my child to an angry, destructive man." When he heard that, he tore up the house and took off for San Diego.

I gather that Cochran said I had phoned Christian in San Diego and asked him to come back, but that's ridiculous. I was staying at the home of my friend Kathy, and I checked my answering machine—Christian had left a message saying it was important that I call him. By the time I reached him it was three A.M. He casually mentioned that he had been out with a girl he had met. This was the man who kept insisting that he wanted us to stay together, who constantly accused me of trying to leave him, and he was telling me that he met a girl. Very strange!

I now realize that Christian constantly confused me with his distorted way of thinking. Candace Garvey told me—and I'm glad she did because it confirmed my judgment—that when she would go to Christian's office he would act differently from day to day. One day he'd say, "I never want to see Faye again!" and the next time she saw him he would say, "I miss her so much I just can't believe it!" And then he wouldn't remember the previous conversation. When Candace would remind him of what he'd said the last time they spoke, he would absolutely deny it.

That is the kind of person I lived with for four years. I now understand what happens in a lot of abusive relationships: Women become so confused that they lose all sense of their own identity and accept their abusers' reality as their own.

I don't blame anyone but myself, but I truly believe that it was the combination of what was happening with Christian, the terrible tension between Nicole and O.J., and my constant fear (maybe it was a premonition) that Nicole's life was in danger that led me back to drugs.

Christian knew that O.J., his idol, used cocaine—O.J. was always very open about it. He told Christian that he had once used pills and had become highly addicted, but he managed to get off them. I don't know whether or not Christian actually saw O.J. do drugs, but—even if he had—I'm sure he would deny it.

O.J.'s use of cocaine was on and off. He often invited Nicole to join him, but she usually refused. He never said where he got it, but he made it clear to me that he always had a supply, and that if I ever wanted any it was readily available. In fact, more than once O.J. said, "Girl, how come you never ask me for any?"

My answer was, "Because I am not doing drugs." And that was the truth at the time.

Chapter 4

DAMAGE AND THE INNER CIRCLE

LOS ANGELES, CALIFORNIA
1994–1995

I think a lot about our friends, Nic's and mine, and all that has happened to us since Nicole's death. In the year since she's been gone, we have often remembered her together. Each of us was initially struck by her beauty, and it became apparent as we grew to know her that her loveliness originated from a strength of character and spirit combined.

For a while she and O.J. appeared to be the ideal couple, but gradually it became obvious to all of us that O.J.'s attention strayed to other women. Nicole tried to ignore it, but we could tell that it hurt her. As I later learned, when she brought it up to him, he became enraged, often blaming his infidelities on her. And sometimes he became so furious and out of control that he beat her.

Despite the fact that O.J. dictated what she would do and when she would do it, where she would go and who she would go with, it was clear that Nicole wanted their marriage to work. She tried desperately to please him and to win his approval, always making excuses for him. She told me on several occasions that O.J. had worked very hard to overcome a sad childhood and now felt he had earned the right to be praised and respected. She also knew that he was very sensitive about his public image and explained that she couldn't blame him if he became angry when he thought she was harming it.

Not only was Nicole the ideal wife and mother, but she was the ideal friend. O.J. liked to have people around and Nicole was a very gracious hostess. She was reserved at first and slow to make friends, but once she did, she was the most considerate, generous, loyal, and loving friend anyone could possibly wish for.

At the time of Nicole's death Cynthia Shahian (CiCi), Robin Greer, Cora Fishman, Kris Jenner, and I saw her most frequently. She had told us all at one time or another that she was afraid that O.J. would kill her.

"O.J. says he is going to kill me and someday he will. And he'll get away with it." She would go on to say that he always felt that he was above the law and he would find a way to put the blame on her. We didn't want to believe her then, but we should have.

Sometimes we talk about what, if anything, we could have done to save her, but we have never been able to come up with an answer that seems to make sense. Her death has been extremely difficult for all of us. Since the verdict, we have all tried to put some type of closure on the year-long fiasco that has essentially turned our lives upside down. As impossible as it is to accept a verdict of not guilty, we all realize we must move on with our lives.

CiCi has told me she still thinks of Nicole often. Having met Nicole and O.J. about fifteen years ago through Kris Jenner and her then-husband, Robert Kardashian, CiCi saw Nicole socially for many years. But it wasn't until after Nicole and O.J. separated that they became quite close.

Although Nicole had told CiCi about O.J.'s abuse in 1992 when they were running together one morning, just five days before Nicole died, Nicole again told CiCi that she was afraid that O.J. would kill her and get away with it. "Just like he did during our divorce," CiCi remembers her saying. "He will charm our friends and family and buy his freedom." CiCi says she'll never forget that conversation. "Nicole was the type of person that didn't speak a lot," CiCi remembers. "When she did, you didn't ask a lot of questions. I told her I would stand by her no matter what and she smiled a little and said, 'Thanks, CiCi,' and we continued our run."

Unfortunately, when CiCi went on the witness stand, the prosecution asked her only about the letter O.J. had written to the Internal Revenue Service hoping Nicole would be put out of her home. Even though the prosecution was aware that CiCi had a great deal of valuable information that could have bolstered their case, it never came out. Immediately after she authenticated the letter, they dismissed her from the stand without questioning her about any of the details they knew she had about Nicole, O.J., and their relationship. I think they had planned to recall her as a rebuttal witness, but for some reason CiCi was never put back on the stand.

Robin Greer had known Nicole the longest, having met Nicole and O.J. while she was dating O.J.'s friend Mark Slotkin, whom she later married and divorced. "Nicole and I were young," Robin says. "Perhaps nineteen or twenty." Robin attended their wedding and Sydney Simpson was named after the character Robin played on the TV soap opera "Ryan's Hope." Robin saw Nicole throughout her relationship with O.J. In the early years she saw how much Nicole adored O.J. Then, like the rest of us, she saw the growing sadness in Nicole's eyes.

When Nicole left O.J. the first time, Robin was working in real estate to supplement her income as an actress and helped find the house on Gretna Green for Nicole and the children. She believes O.J. never forgave her for helping Nicole.

Like me, Robin feels her life has been shattered by Nicole's death. She had known Nic for fifteen years, so they had been close friends for most of their adult lives. When she was married to Mark Slotkin, Robin got to know O.J.'s golfing buddies— "the O.J. worshippers" is what she called them—so she had a somewhat unique perspective on some of the players in the case. Robin also was friendly with A.C. Immediately after the murder A.C. contacted her to see if she would swallow the drug cartel theory. Robin, the comedian of the group, laughed and said, "Right, A.C. They were meeting with the Colombian cartel between taking Sydney to dance class and Justin to karate. Or was it before taking Francesca to Catholic school? I think not!"

When I asked her how it felt to see her ex-husband defend O.J. publicly on television, she said it didn't surprise her a bit—Mark would walk over hot coals for O.J. In fact, he seemed willing to walk over her, as well. When Mark got wind of Robin talking to the prosecution, he told her he knew she needed money and if she would retract her statement he was sure he could help her out financially. Robin's response was, "If I was after money, I could make a fortune telling the truth, so why should I lie?"

Robin could not be bought, and she continued to tell the truth every chance she had. After making her position clear to both A.C. and Mark, she was told that if she continued to defame O.J., her life would not be worth a cent. They would make sure that no one would believe a word she had to say. They also reminded her that as an actress her career was based on public opinion, so if she ever wanted to work again she had better get smart.

After *Private Diary* was published, O.J. and the boys started their smear campaign against her through the talk show circuit, but it didn't work. Robin had a number of very powerful friends, socially and in the press, who were able to put out the flames before they became wildfires.

When we were discussing the behavior of O.J.'s golf buddies after they began to realize that O.J. might be guilty, she said, "They knew he was guilty all along—they had just decided to turn a blind eye to what O.J. did. But with all the evidence that came in, it would have been socially unacceptable to continue the charade." Then she asked me if I had noticed the mass exodus from the courtroom that had occurred. Suddenly there were few of O.J.'s friends there to support him.

Robin was convinced that it would take an act of God for the jury to convict O.J. because the trial had become even more convoluted after the Fuhrman tapes were released. I disagreed emphatically. Interestingly enough, Robin also had nightmares of being murdered.

Robin's first reaction to Nicole's death was to isolate herself. She hated being inundated by reporters at this most painful time, and seeing O.J.'s arrogant attitude immobilized her with frustration. Also, the man Robin was seeing at the time of Nicole's death chose to distance himself from her to avoid being brought into the limelight.

It was Robin who brought Linda Schulman to the attention of the prosecution. Although she was never part of our group, Linda was one of Nicole's best friends—they were very close for at least ten years of the time that Nicole was with O.J. Linda had seen Nicole covered with bruises many times, and Nicole had told her exactly where they had come from, so Linda knew all about the beatings and the other ways that O.J. had abused her. She also knew about the time six or seven years before Nicole's death when O.J. had beaten Nicole so severely with a wine bottle that she had ended up in the hospital with broken ribs and bruises all over her stomach. O.J. had instructed Nicole to tell the doctor that she had fallen off her bicycle. The doctor who treated Nicole at that time was willing to testify that Nicole was badly injured and that it definitely was not from falling off a bicycle, but the prosecution did not call him, nor did they call Linda.

I'm thankful that the laws are now changing in some states to require doctors to report injuries they see that may be the result of domestic violence.

Robin, CiCi, and I never stopped being supportive of one another, although other friends had some problems about where they stood. Initially Kris and Bruce Jenner both seemed to understand my reasons for publishing *Private Diary.* When I first told Bruce that I was very nervous about telling all that I knew, "You just tell the truth," he said, "and the truth shall set you free."

But when I saw Kris and Bruce shortly after *Private Diary* was published, they seemed to be singing a different tune.

"You told me to tell the truth, and I did."

"Yes," Bruce said, "but we had no idea how much truth there was."

"Not many people did," I answered, knowing that they were both uncomfortable that I had written so many intimate details about Nicole and the rest of us.

"Please look at it from another viewpoint," I later begged Kris, who remains one of my dearest friends. "This is not about disgracing our friend Nicole. You know that Nicole would want us to do everything we could to save other women from living through the kind of torment she endured and ending up as she did." And I reminded her that long before I wrote the first word, practically every detail of our lives had been in the tabloids— probably more than once. So if I had not told the whole truth, the readers would not have known what was honest, what I had left out, and what I was covering up.

My friends soon understood that although I had agreed to write the book to protect my life, it was also because I wanted to reveal the true facts about Nicole's murder. And I was determined to warn abused women everywhere that the same thing could happen to them.

Candace Garvey also had reservations at first. But as she became aware of the reasons I had written the book and the way it was helping others, she became my staunch ally. Because their daughter was in the same dance recital as Sydney Simpson, Candace and Steve Garvey saw O.J. there the night of the murders. At the trial, Candace testified for the prosecution that O.J. seemed to be in a very strange and despondent mood that evening—that he seemed preoccupied and remote, almost as if he had been drugged. Candace spoke with such dignity and integrity that I wanted to cry because I had been hearing so many lies in that trial. When I later asked her how she felt about testifying, she said she just hoped that she had made a difference.

She has the same dreams as Robin and I do. She told me, "Sometimes I wake up from a nightmare that O.J. was trying to find me or had just killed me. It doesn't happen often, but it always seems to come back when I least expect it. I guess it's the closest I'll ever come to an understanding of what it was like for Nicole—the terrible fear that O.J. would kill her, and being unable to get away from him."

She said, "I think of Nicole so often. Not only do I mourn the loss of a friend, but her death changed my outlook on many things. I can no longer pretend not to see cruelty or abuse. And I will never again stand by and let a friend suffer in silence.

"The 'trial of the century' was very painful for me," Candace added. "It became a long-winded miniseries that was more about the attorneys and the Los Angeles Police Department than about Ron or Nicole. I hate to think that money can buy justice or, in my opinion, injustice. Even if the jury's decision is that O.J. is not guilty, those of us who know the truth will know that they were wrong."

Although Nicole spent time with her family on major holidays and other family occasions and she loved them very much, she sometimes felt that O.J. had them in his corner.

O.J. was always generous, but Nicole felt there were strings attached. The Browns were grateful to him for jobs, vacations, tuition, and other kinds of support. Consequently, anytime Nicole went to her family when O.J. had beaten or mistreated her, they would try to comfort her, but then they would say something like, "You're being too hard on him. Just think of all he does for you." And Juditha, "Dita" as he called her, was O.J.'s confidante. They were on the phone practically every day and Juditha seemed somehow seduced by him. So Nicole always knew that by the time she talked to her mother, Juditha would have already heard O.J.'s side of every argument.

I am still puzzled by what happened when I sent the Browns money for Sydney and Justin's education. My check for $10,000 from the proceeds of *Diary* went to them with a letter stating that it was to be used for the children's education and that I would be sending more. I was informed that there would not be a fund for the education of Nicole's children, and that all contributions were going to the Nicole Brown Simpson Charitable Foundation. They cashed the check, but when I learned that the money would not be earmarked for Sydney and Justin, I decided to send my future donations to groups and organizations that help or help educate victims of domestic violence.

Right after I left Exodus, Denise Brown called me and said, "I would like you to answer the media's questions about Nicole. We're not able to. We have too much grief right now. So we're asking her friends to do that for us."

I told Denise that I'd do anything in the world for Nicole and her family but added, "However, there is a problem: Robert Kardashian is making sure that as many people as possible know that I just got out of Exodus Recovery Center. I gather that he's hoping that nobody will believe anything I have to say."

"Faye, that doesn't matter," she said. "You were very close to Nicole and you knew and understood her. I think that's what's really important."

"When and if I speak out, I plan to tell the whole story," I replied.

"What are you talking about?" Denise asked, sounding a little wary.

"I plan to tell all about the abuse that Nicole went through."

"We are not talking about abuse!" she shouted and hung up the phone.

That was when I realized that the Browns were having great difficulty in facing the truth.

A November 23, 1994, article in the *Orange County Register* reported:

Hours after the slashing death of Nicole Brown Simpson, her older sister yelled into the telephone at Simpson: "You murderer. You killed my sister. You always said you were going to do it."

"He said, 'Me?' That's all he thinks about is me, me, me," Denise Brown *said in an interview with the* Register. *It was the first time she had publicly condemned Mr. Simpson as the killer of her sister and Ronald Goldman. Ms. Brown said previously that her sister had been a battered wife and questioned why the defense sought to suppress evidence if Mr. Simpson was innocent.*

This news suprised me since initially Denise went on television with Diane Sawyer and told the world that her sister was not a battered woman and she was amazed to hear people suggest such a thing.

Nevertheless, I was pleased that Denise had the courage to take the stand and speak honestly about memories that were extremely painful. She told about the time O.J. had thrown Nicole out the door, and about one of his favorite ways to humiliate her: O.J. would walk up to Nicole, grab her crotch, and say, "This is mine, this is where babies come from," and sometimes he would continue on in more graphic detail. And that's how O.J. treated Nicole even when he wasn't angry with her.

Cora Fishman, another friend of Nicole's, also grew quite strange following the murders and throughout the trial. She and Nicole jogged together in the mornings and Cora was around her fairly often.

I was friendly with Cora, but we never became really good friends. I knew that her husband adored her and showered her with extravagant gifts. And there were periods when she seemed content and was able to be a loving wife and a concerned mother to her children. Then suddenly a cloud would seem to descend over her.

Although she used Nicole as her excuse for being out until all hours almost every night in the week, Cora wasn't around much the last few months of Nicole's life. She was spending every possible moment with a young man who had captivated her fancy.

Even though I had no illusions about Cora, I was sick when I heard that she went on one of the tabloid TV shows bad-mouthing Nicole. She implied that Nicole was a party girl, and it appeared from her various statements that she sympathized with O.J.

Of course, no one can understand the reasons for the behavior of anyone else. We were all in an overwhelming situation. We had lost our best friend to a vicious murder and we knew that the murderer was in our circle of friends.

I am not trying to make excuses for Cora, because there's no earthly excuse for her behavior. Supposedly she was Nicole's very close and loyal friend and true friends stand up for each other. It was disappointing and painful for our group to see Cora being persuaded and manipulated by O.J.

No matter what O.J. did to Nicole, Cora always told her she should stay with him. That bothered me very much because it was so obvious that

Nicole needed to get away. She used to say to Nicole, "So every now and then you get beaten. What's the big deal? You have everything you want with that man. You have a mansion, you can have any car you want to drive, and you have security forever." When Nicole told Cora that she was afraid O.J. was going to kill her, Cora's answer was, "It's a figment of your imagination." Cora may not admit it, but I imagine that she may regret encouraging Nicole to stay with O.J., even at the very end.

Ron and Cora Fishman have had a strained, on-and-off relationship for a very long time—it's difficult to explain. In some respects she does as she pleases, but he still controls her in many ways. I saw that happening when I was talking to Ron right after Nicole died.

He said, "Faye, when the investigators for the prosecution start calling you, remember that omitting information is not the same as lying."

I looked at him, not understanding. "Could you explain that a little bit further?"

He said that even though he knew a great deal about the relationship between O.J. and Nicole and the night Nicole was killed, he wasn't about to ruin his life over it. He added that anybody who talked too much about it might never be the same.

He went on to explain that, for my own sake, if I went on the witness stand I should not even mention O.J.'s death threats.

I could see that Ron was still in shock. I said, "Ron, what happened that night? I know you were with O.J. at Sydney's recital. Candace Garvey and Nicole said he was in a bizarre, dark mood. Did you see that?"

His answer was, "To be honest with you, O.J. was pretty angry. His exact words were, 'I'm not finished with her. I'm gonna get her, but good.'"

"Are you planning to tell that to the prosecution?" I asked. "That's the kind of information they need—it explains his state of mind."

He quickly replied, "Of course not! O.J. is my friend and there's nothing we can do about the murders now. Nicole is dead—we can't change that. But we can certainly save our own lives and our own reputations."

"Ron," I said, "I'm really sorry to disagree with you. I believe in truth and in loyalty to a friend. The fact that we can't change what happened doesn't excuse us. You know very well that silence is agreement. If I were to be silent or omit information that could lead to the truth, I would lose my self-respect and I would never be able to live with myself."

I am sure Cora Fishman would not have had any problem helping the defense by testifying that O.J. Simpson was a saint. Poor Cora became so confused that she no longer knew what day it was.

Before I had decided whether I would go through with writing *Private Diary*, Cora suggested that she should co-author it with me. I told her frankly that it just did not feel right to me. Then I heard that she was going to write her own book, but I gather that it did not work out for her. When she learned I had written the book without her, Cora may have felt resentful. I also believe that her lashing out at me and Nicole may have been due to frustration and the pressure O.J. was putting on her and Ron. Whatever the cause, she became very hostile to me and others in our group.

For Cora to go on television and say that Nicole had been behaving like a twenty-year-old party girl was completely unwarranted. Cora knew that Nicole had been a good and faithful wife to O.J., and that she was always an incredibly conscientious mother to her children. Anyway, since Nicole and O.J. were divorced, Nicole had every right to go out when and with whom she wished. She had not dated in seventeen years and she needed to do what she could to get over the terrible times with O.J. and probably O.J. himself. For the first time since she was seventeen, Nicole could live her life without having her every move controlled by O.J. She was like a bird let out of a cage and she wanted to fly free. She needed to make her own decisions and wanted O.J. to stop dictating what she could or could not do. She probably was acting like most other women do who have ever been in an abusive relationship for that long, but Cora made it sound as if Nicole's behavior was outrageous.

What gave Cora Fishman the right to judge Nicole? Cora was the one who had always said to Nicole, "Let's go dancing, let's go here, let's go there. . . ." Then, there she was on national television condemning Nicole for doing just that.

Unfortunately Nicole told Cora about the night she and I had slept together, and Cora couldn't wait to spread the word after Nicole's death. Nicole trusted Cora and confided in her, and only her, about that night. Not only did Cora violate that confidence, she made it into something that it never was. By the time she had spread it around, a onetime experience sounded like a longtime gay relationship. If Cora had not felt so compelled to talk about it, it could have remained an insignificant matter that never would have been disclosed. Instead it reached the tabloids and I had no alternative but to write about it in *Private Diary*.

After Nicole and I had slept together, I told her, "I have never done anything like that in my life. It was something that could happen only once. I don't regret it, but I feel that it is a part of my life that should never be discussed with anyone." I am still surprised that Nicole decided to tell Cora, but I'm sure it never occurred to her that Cora could not be trusted.

Soon after Nicole's death Cora came up to me and said, "I know that you and Nicole spent that night together." It took me a minute to understand what she meant, but then I felt that she was trying to blackmail me. I said, "Cora, please, just forget it. It doesn't have any bearing on anything, so for the sake of my daughter and Nicole's children, let it go. And for Nicole's sake, it is something that should not be discussed."

Cora's response was, "Well, I just know it's going to come out."

I could only say, "How could it come out unless you were to talk about it?"

It is my impression that Cora told Ron, then Ron and Cora told O.J. It soon spread to everyone in our group, and I started getting phone calls from my friends, saying, "Why didn't you tell me about what happened between you and Nicole?"

Ron also told Christian and he started quizzing me on the details. Before another day had passed,

I realized everyone in our circle had been told. I knew that many of these people were planning to defend O.J. and would use that episode against Nicole and me.

I was sick at the thought of what that information would do to my child and Nicole's children, as well as Nicole's and my reputations, but I knew that I had to tell the truth. Not only for the integrity of the book, but because I did not want the embellished versions that were going around to be accepted as fact.

One of the most difficult things I have ever had to do was explain to Francesca what was going to be said—what was already being said. I told her that her Aunt Nicole and I had spent a night together, and that it was something that had never happened before and would never have happened again. I tried to tell her as gently, lovingly, and honestly as possible, without going into detail. I'm sure she understood—in this day and age, children know much more than we would imagine.

Months after *Private Diary* was published I went to pick up Francesca at the house of one of her friends who lived on Rockingham not far from Cora. As I was leaving the driveway, my car was blocked. It was Cora. She came dashing over to us and said, "We must talk. I was so confused and I have been terribly misunderstood. Nicole would be very sad to know that the friends she loved most have grown so far apart."

I thought, *Sure, you were so confused that you couldn't wait to talk to the press,* but I merely said, "Cora, you should have thought of that earlier—I can't ease your conscience."

I tried to leave, but she wanted to continue the conversation. I pointed out that my daughter was in the car and that this was not anything she needed to hear. She said, "I really need to talk to you."

I said, "Call me if you wish." I got a call from her, but I did not return it.

I tried very hard to protect Francesca from having to take the brunt of my notoriety. Fortunately she was in a wonderful Catholic school that kept her very well insulated from all the gossip. The parents of a number of the children in the school were Nicole's friends, so they must have been aware of what was going on, but the teachers made it clear that there would be no talk about anyone or anything pertaining to the O.J. Simpson case.

I also tried to keep Francesca from watching television reports about the trial, and I made sure that she was with children who would understand that we did not ever talk about it. But despite all our efforts, she heard some of the reports. I know that I put a lot on my child, but she has come through it like a champ.

When I told her that I was going to write the book, I said, "Francesca, this is what we're up against: Your Aunt Nicole has been murdered and I need to tell the truth about it. I want you to know what's in store for us." And I explained that even if I did not write the book, there would be attacks on me, that in fact they had already started. I told her that I wanted to warn women that they could not stay with men who were very mean and tried to hurt them.

As young as she was, Francesca was already very interested in helping others. She was, as always, very loving and she agreed that it would be okay for us to be apart for a while if that was what it would take for me to try to make a difference in the lives of women who might be in danger.

She was very supportive and said, "Well, Mommy, if that is going to help other women and stop some of them from getting hurt or killed, then we have to do it." I am very proud of her for that. She is a wise child with common sense well beyond her eleven years. I am grateful to be able to say that so far Francesca is doing fine.

PART II

Media Madness

Now I know how it feels to be up against the media. When I was being interviewed about Private Diary *and something would come up about Faye, I could sense the attitude, "This is a woman with a great body who once used drugs."*

When I explained, "Faye Resnick is really a decent, sincere person who has a story to tell and is trying very hard to help abused women," I'd think I had made my point. The next day I'd read a column that said, "Faye Resnick is a woman with a great body who once used drugs."

—Mike Walker, *National Enquirer* columnist
and co-author of *Private Diary*

Chapter 5

PUBLICATION DAY

STOWE, VERMONT
OCTOBER 18, 1994

*I*t was the publication day of *Private Diary,* and I
knew I should be excited, but I was too numb to
feel anything. I still did not have the energy to
read the papers or watch the news. I wanted to
hide and continue to recover from the loss of my
best friend and the strange aftermath of pain, lies,
and confusion coming from the O.J. camp, the
media, and others. There was also considerable
strain from working on the book and having to
relive the memories of Nicole's pain and her death.

After a few weeks of rest in France, I returned
to Vermont, where Mike Walker, my collaborator,
and I had written the book, to prepare myself for
the onslaught of the press. It wasn't long before

countless members of the media (who had never met or even spoken with me) had assured the public that I had one and only one motive: money.

O.J. Simpson was on trial for murdering Nicole and Ron Goldman. Nicole had told me and her other close friends that O.J. had said he would kill her and that he would get away with it. And in the weeks before the murders he called me many times saying that he was going to kill her. Now O.J. and his defense team—including Johnnie Cochran, Robert Shapiro, and my former friend Robert Kardashian—were doing all they could to further the impression that I was a profiteer and to convince the world I was a hopeless drug addict and an irresponsible liar.

I had told the truth in my book and I had hoped that the public would hear my side of the story, but I was beginning to see that despite my hopes and intentions, this would be an uphill struggle.

I was sick of hearing about O.J. Simpson. Every television station was having newsbreaks about O.J. this and O.J. that, so I avoided the major stations and watched the TV channel that shows old movies. I was half watching a film I had seen at least six times before, trying to be peaceful and to center myself, when suddenly there was a newsbreak, something I did not expect on that channel: "The trial of the century has been stopped over a book." At that moment the phone rang. It was Michael Viner, the president of Dove Books. "Faye," he said, "Judge Ito has stopped the trial in order to read your book."

I was speechless but knew then that it had been worth all the false accusations, unjust criticism, and intense work I had gone through. The phone rang every two minutes for the rest of the day. Maybe we all hope to make a contribution in our lives, but never expect to be in the eye of the storm. Little did I know the storm had just begun.

Chapter 6

MEET THE PRESS

CONNIE CHUNG

I originally had met and spoken with Connie Chung informally right after finishing the book in September. Remembering how gracious she had been during that meeting, I felt relatively relaxed at the beginning of our television interview. However, her tone quickly changed and I found myself being attacked by invasive, rather hostile questions about drugs, my lifestyle, and everything on which she could place a negative or controversial spin.

After a while, I said, "Stop!"

Connie said, "What's wrong?"

"I am trying to make a point about domestic violence. You have not asked me one question about that and you have not asked me any question that is relevant to what we agreed we'd talk about. I am trying to make a difference. I am a woman who wants to help other women and I was told that you were, too. If you want to continue this interview, we have to go on that basis."

Connie did not say anything and I walked out. Michael Viner took me aside and said, "You know, if you walk out, she's going to air that. She will use that and you will look as if you couldn't handle the pressure."

So I walked back inside and said, "Connie, could we have an understanding? I really cannot sit here and be assaulted like that."

Her answer was, "Faye, you know those questions would have been asked by anyone who interviewed you."

I said, "You are right, some of the questions would have been asked, but not over and over. Please understand that if we continue, when I have answered a question once, I will not answer it again. And if I feel something is totally irrelevant or that I am being exploited, I will tell you or I will not answer the question."

Connie said, "Okay." And for the rest of the interview she was very pleasant. However, I had asked her not to do any close-ups because my hair was now olive green from a hair-coloring fiasco in France and I knew I looked terrible. Of course, the camera ended up being inches from my face.

When I left Connie, I went to my hotel room feeling absolutely disheartened. A little later Michael called. "That was something, wasn't it?"

"I don't know if I'm going to be able to do this," I said. "I really don't know how to respond when I am attacked like that. She seemed so understanding when we met. I knew she would have to ask some tough questions, but I had expected her to be more of a woman's woman and less of a shark."

I went to sleep that night thinking, *How am I going to continue this?* I was very concerned about how that interview would turn out because at that point I really did not trust Connie at all. And I knew that interviews can be edited so that you come out saying something totally different from what you really meant.

When the program was aired, Connie had edited out the majority of her attack on me, and during the introduction she said, "Faye Resnick is becoming the most famous author in the world and she would like to let the world know that between two and four million women are abused every year."

I was very grateful for that. So even though it was difficult, the final result was a very good interview from Connie's point of view, and a very constructive one from mine.

MAURY POVICH

The next day I was scheduled to be on "The Maury Povich Show." They sent a car for us, and Michael Viner and I went to the set. It was a friendly, caring place, very busy, very New York. The people seemed genuinely creative and they seemed to enjoy working together.

It started out very pleasantly. Michael and I were in a private office instead of the green room, and they brought us a great assortment of wonderful delicacies to enjoy while we waited.

Maury came in and Michael introduced us. I really liked him. He said, "I saw some of the clips last night with my wife. I hope you feel secure and comfortable about them. I think it will be a great interview."

I said, "We'll see, Maury," thinking to myself, *If this interview turns out to be like what happened with Connie Chung, I will just walk away and not explain anything, and I won't care what anybody says. They can buy the book and read it if they want to, and at this point I don't care if they don't.*

When we went on the set, I was surprised to see how many people there were in the studio. It was a very mixed group—male and female, young and old, black and white.

Maury started by asking me questions. He was gentle and for a while we had a very comfortable and, I thought, rather good conversation. Then the producer of the show decided it was time to get some audience participation.

I really wasn't prepared for what happened next because I had not had a clue there was going to be an audience there. Before I walked on the set, I was told that a few people would ask a couple of questions. I said, "Please, I don't know how to deal with that. I'm not an actress. This is all new to me." They assured me it would be fine, so I said a couple of questions would be okay with me. All I wanted to do was get to the subject of domestic violence.

The first moment that Maury opened it up to the audience I could sense a great deal of hostility coming from some of the crowd. When I started answering questions about O.J. abusing Nicole, they all jumped in at the same time, saying things like, "Who is Faye Resnick? What makes her think she knows so much?" and "She's a phony! She probably didn't even know Nicole." There was real hatred in the air. It was frightening!

Someone has since suggested that perhaps agitators had been planted in the audience. Knowing what I now know about O.J.'s defense team, that's perfectly within the realm of possibility. There were a couple of very angry women in the crowd who just sneered at everything I said. I tried to make it clear that I was telling what I knew, and it was up to them to decide whether or not to believe me—all to no avail.

I tried to stay calm and explain that I could only tell the truth as I knew it. I said I knew I couldn't change their opinions and that I understood that it might be very confusing for them because they had not lived through it as I had. But, I said, I had seen O.J. inflict psychological abuse on Nicole time and again, and she had told me about the physical abuse. I also told them I had seen O.J. go into rages, absolute rages, and had gone through all that with Nicole.

We have to remember that nobody there had heard the true facts at that time and they all thought I was lying. The family was still saying that Nicole was not battered, so I could understand why it might be easy to believe that I was just out there trying to make money out of a fantasy I had created.

Then Maury touched a nerve of every member of the audience: "In *Private Diary,* you talked about O.J. telling you that he would murder Nicole." That's when the audience really flipped out! When they quieted down enough to hear me, I asked, "What do you need, a video of him killing her? Would that satisfy you?"

That seemed to be what the world needed to believe O.J. was the murderer—a video of O.J. slitting Nicole's throat. And even then, there are many who still would not believe it. When I said, "I understand how you feel—this is your hero," they said, "No, it's not that he's our hero, it's that you're a liar."

I guess I shouldn't have taken the insults and hostility to heart. But I did. The ugly things I was accused of, the talk of profiteering, all of the misinformation that was put out about me hurt me deeply. I try to appear strong, and I am in certain ways, but in reality I am as vulnerable as the next person.

Until Nicole's terrible death, the last thing I had ever contemplated doing was defending Nicole, defending the truth, and standing up to fight against domestic violence. It was not what I had planned, but it had to be done and no one else was doing it. The lies were coming from every direction—from Nicole's family, O.J.'s buddies, the defense, and the tabloids. I was the person telling the truth, but they did not want to hear it.

During one of the breaks I left the set to pull myself together. Maury had been asking questions about the battering and tears were streaming down my face. I did not know if I could find the strength to go on with it. Then I saw Michael Viner sitting right in the front row. He was looking at me as if to say, "Oh Faye, I'm so sorry. I didn't have a clue that it would be like this." And I went back on the set.

I was under the impression that it was going to be a half-hour show and I was sitting there thinking that this half hour was turning into a year. I was attacked more severely than I could have ever imagined, but I believe I stood my ground. It was a very tough hour. And I realized that it was time for me to learn to be tough, too. I made my point very loud and clear: O.J. Simpson was a murderer, and no man should ever be able to get away with abusing a woman as he had abused Nicole.

It was also during this show that I sensed a great deal of hostility because I was not a "working woman." "Tell me how you and Nicole spent your days, Faye," Maury asked.

"We would get our children up and dressed, we would make their breakfast and take them to school. Then we might meet some friends and have a cappuccino. Or maybe we'd play some tennis." (Because I was so nervous, I did not think to mention that I also had worked a couple of hours a day for Christian, that I would often work for one charitable cause or another, and that we would pick our children up, make dinner, do their homework with them, and get them to bed.)

Maury looked at me as if I were from another planet and some of the people in the audience looked very disapproving. "That's how you live?" Maury asked incredulously.

"We knew we were fortunate and had very nice lives," I answered. "We tried to use our time to help others in ways that women who worked might not be able to. We volunteered on campaigns for better schools, fund-raisers for charities, and a variety of causes." I felt I was being attacked for being "only a mother" and not having a full-time job.

Chapter 7

VERMONT INCOGNITO

*A*fter the Connie Chung and Maury Povich interviews, I returned to Vermont to collect myself and prepare for other interviews. The book hadn't been out for two days, yet the media attention had grown heated and intense, making it almost impossible to go anywhere. Even getting to the house was an ordeal. Michael Viner and I had to call from the plane to arrange to be picked up and were told that the property was surrounded by newshounds from "Hard Copy" and "A Current Affair" who kept coming to the door trying to find out if I was there.

When we landed at the Burlington airport, we got in the car for the forty-five-minute drive to the house. About ten minutes before we arrived I had to climb onto the floor of the car and be covered with a blanket so no one could see that I was arriving. When we got to the house, I had to sneak in under the same blanket. I felt like a criminal, but I needed some time alone and I did not want my privacy to be invaded by the press. I'd had more than enough for a while.

Just after *Private Diary* came out, a *Los Angeles Times* article was published slamming me and every word I had written. It was a rather long article and although it did have a few positive words at the end, I believe that responsible journalism is about balance. Their story was loaded with paragraphs demeaning me and the book. Of course, many people in the media are O.J.'s buddies and big members of his fan club. Like the *Los Angeles Times*, NBC's West Coast president, Don Ohlmeyer, was pro O.J. and therefore hesitant to believe me. People like Ohlmeyer have real clout with broadcasters, network affiliates throughout the country, and members of the press.

It took close to a year but eventually the *Los Angeles Times* changed their tune. In July, right after I was subpoenaed by the defense, they interviewed me and allowed me to make my points and, although it was long overdue—a year after Nicole's death—the story was fair.

Back in Vermont right after the book was published, however, fairness was in no one's vocabulary. The press was having a feeding frenzy and *Private Diary* and I were considered fair game. I tried to ignore it, but Michael Viner recommended I make some attempt to see what was going on. So I started watching the news programs and some of the tell-all shows. I was sorry I had when some man on the "Geraldo" show said he used to do drugs with me and called me a "strawberry"—a term for a woman who would do anything for drugs.

I had tuned in late so I had to call the "Geraldo" show to find out the man's name. I had never even heard of him! That's how crazy it became. Absolute strangers were selling stories about me that they had fabricated out of thin air.

Geraldo later said that he had found out that the man was a total liar and that he would make a public apology. I was told he did, but he also replayed that segment on a subsequent show. Much later Geraldo made a great point of apologizing several times, admitting publicly how right I had been about many issues regarding the O.J. trial.

The last thing I wanted was to see all those shows. Although it was helpful to know what people were saying so I could respond to the lies, it was troubling to witness the wide array of strangers telling such incredible tales. During this time, however, I also saw the media picking up on what I'd said about O.J.'s abuse of Nicole and domestic violence in general. What I had written was beginning to get attention and I was extremely hopeful about the effect of the book when I heard it had reached number one on the *New York Times* bestseller list. Reporters were trying to contact me, but I didn't want to plan any more interviews just yet. I was still trying to recover, reeling from the fact that pretty much without exception the media had painted me as the profiteer of the century, and I had no interest in further fueling that fire.

For the record, *Private Diary* did not make me a rich woman. Even if it had, countless journalists and reporters have been well paid to write about every angle and facet of the O.J. Simpson case. The criticism seemed unfair when, in fact, I was the one who knew the truth and was trying to set the record straight.

During that month in Vermont I met with two investigators from the Los Angeles District Attorney's office who needed a lot of details that we had not had time to get into in Los Angeles.

I also met with David Margolick of the *New York Times*, a journalist I have come to respect very much and who helped restore my faith in at least some members of the press. He came to Stowe for a day and stayed for dinner that night. It was a pleasure to talk with him about how writing the book had affected my life. The result was an article that appeared in the *New York Times* in November called "A Prisoner of Her Own Book," a perfect title considering that's exactly how I felt.

Of course, I was in Vermont, a very beautiful and serene prison, but I couldn't go out, I couldn't do anything. I couldn't even go to the grocery store because everywhere I went, people knew who I was, and I did not want the press breathing down my neck. I was walking around wearing hoods and scarves and sunglasses, and at one point I even tried to cover my face. It was ridiculous and I was getting depressed. At that time, though, mail began coming in from women who had read *Private Diary*. Not only were there letters of support and appreciation, but more importantly there were also letters from women who were leaving abusive relationships after reading Nicole's book. This development made my travails well worth it. I was committed to moving forward.

Chapter 8

ROMANTIC REUNION?

LOS ANGELES, CALIFORNIA
OCTOBER 1994

*A*fter the book was launched and the early
interviews on the East Coast were complete, it
was time to go home to Los Angeles. Although I
had had time to heal, I had been away from my
daughter too long, and I was anxious to return
home. Because it was important that the media
and the defense team not know I had returned, I
stayed at a hotel. In the end, it was a wasted effort
because I was stupid enough to talk to Christian
Reichardt, my former fiancé, who found it fitting
to share this information with the people I was
trying to avoid.

Christian had left numerous messages for me
saying how much he loved me and that he really

wanted to see me. I should have ignored him, but after being sequestered in Vermont for what felt like forever, I was lonely. So, exactly like Nicole and the abused women I have been working with over the past year, I weakened and returned his call. He was at his most charming and, although I had promised myself that I would have nothing more to do with him, I told him that I was at the Century Towers and agreed that he could come there that evening.

I took a long, lazy bath, did my hair carefully, and put on my favorite silk pajamas. Even though I did not want to be, I was excited at the thought of seeing him again. He walked in, took me in his arms, and told me that he had never stopped loving me, not even for a minute. He held me tenderly as he apologized over and over for having let me down. I had dinner sent up from room service and by the time it was over, I was falling under his spell again.

When I awakened after a night that rekindled the passion I had once felt for him—in bed at least—Christian was propped up against the pillows reading *Private Diary*. He must have been at it for a while because he was quite far into it and seemed to be completely absorbed. While he had his coffee, I read parts of it to him. He was very gentle and loving, and talked about how we could rebuild our lives together. After breakfast he left for his office, saying that he could hardly wait to get back to me and was looking forward to reading the rest of the book and spending more time with me.

When Christian returned that evening, there was something subtly different about him. That first night, except for his telling me how much he loved me and how close we would be, we hadn't talked about much of anything. He still acted as if everything was okay, but I could sense that he was different. Making love with Christian had always been fantastic, but that night I couldn't get over the feeling that I was sleeping with the enemy.

The following morning I knew that was just what I had done when he tried to get me to retract some of the things I had said in the book. A little later, after Christian had left for the office, Michael Viner called and told me about an interview Christian was going to do with Barbara Walters.

"Everything I have written was the truth, so why would I go back on any of it?" I told Christian when he returned that evening. "I would be lying, and I am not willing to do that."

"You wrote terrible things about O.J.," Christian yelled. "I have no idea what you're talking about." When I repeated that every word in the book was absolutely true, he said he had never seen O.J. behave as I said he had. To jog Christian's memory, I reminded him of the night at the California Beach Sushi restaurant when O.J. became so drunk and frenzied that the manager asked us to leave, the police were called, and the policemen said that Nicole was to go home with us.

Christian flatly denied it, saying O.J. was "just a little upset."

I said, "The manager will tell you that what I said about that evening was exactly what happened." I was learning that Christian would protect O.J. at any price. And it began to dawn on me that "price" was the key word. Christian then repeated what he had said before I had left town to write the book: "I have a story to tell about abused men, and about how you and Nicole abused me and O.J."

I said, "I didn't understand you the first time you said that and I still don't know what you're talking about."

He started in again about how Nicole and I used to go dancing. I said, "Wait a minute, Christian, you encouraged us to go and how often did that happen . . . maybe four times? Most of the time you joined us. Then, all of a sudden, when O.J. didn't want Nicole out of his sight, you decided that it was not okay for me to go out, either."

He just said, "Well, you guys abused us. I have a story to tell and I'm going to tell it!"

That's when I said, "Christian, I had a phone call from Michael Viner telling me that you have an interview set up with Barbara Walters."

Before that, he had been saying things like, "We need to trust each other and tell each other every single detail," and "It's important for us to be totally honest and open with each other."

I said, "Why didn't you tell me about the interview?"

"It's none of your business," he snapped.

"Oh, everything that I say and do is your business, but nothing you say and do is any of mine. That's what has gone on for four years now, but it will not go on any longer. I am through hearing your apologies and I am through being confused by you."

I suddenly understood what he had been trying to do and I told him to get out of my life. At first he did not believe me, and when I insisted that he leave, he became very ugly and destructive. He started smashing the furniture and tried to pin me against the wall.

I was terrified, so the minute he was out the door I called a friend and said, "Christian just left. He has torn up the hotel room and pushed me around." An attorney was immediately sent over to document what had happened.

It marked the end of my illusions about Christian and the beginning of my disillusionment about the media.

* * *

Christian had told me that O.J. kept calling him from jail. I knew that Christian never changed the code on his answering machine and I wanted to hear what O.J. had in mind. So I checked the messages on his machine and heard more than enough. "Get all the information out of her that you can, and see if you can confuse her," O.J. said. "Convince people that her book is a pack of lies." When it finally dawned on me that Christian was working for O.J., I thought, *Oh my God, this guy is owned!*

That day Christian did his interview with Barbara Walters, who had more than enough information on Christian's background to conduct a balanced interview. But she seemed willing to let him sit there and tell lie after lie to the American public.

When she asked Christian if I was doing drugs the night of one of O.J.'s threats to kill Nicole, he said he didn't know, but added that drugs always impair the memory and anyone who has ever done drugs will never again be able to remember anything clearly.

Isn't it interesting that she didn't question Christian on how many times, if any, he saw me using drugs, or the fact that he used drugs himself? Considering that Walters is close to Robert Shapiro, I suppose that's not surprising. Shapiro apparently had set up the interview to be a kill piece on me.

When I heard his interview, I was heartsick. It was so obvious that O.J. was able to get Christian to tell outright lies for him. I felt betrayed and knew it would be a very long time before I would ever be able to trust another man. I called Christian and left what I thought was my final message to him: "You have now gone on national television and lied for a murderer. Please remember that I want nothing to do with you ever again. You have joined the darkness. I want to stay in the light, so I cannot even speak with anyone like you."

I have since learned that Christian told others that I was on drugs during the time O.J. called to tell me that he would kill Nicole. So he went from saying he didn't know if I was doing drugs to saying I was so drugged that I couldn't possibly have known what I had heard. He also said that I was close to Nicole for only three months—another outright lie. But he did not stop there.

In August, when I saw Christian testifying for the defense, I was spiritually wounded. Here was a man who knew the truth but told one lie after another. I kept hoping for truth and conviction to overtake him, knowing full well it was impossible at that point. He was too far gone.

As he sat on the stand in the suit I had bought for him, wearing the Rolex watch I had given to him for his birthday just one year earlier, I couldn't help but wonder what ungodly spirit had taken over this person I had once loved. He had professed to be so spiritual—how could he have joined the dark side so quickly? What could have happened to make him sell his soul?

During the direct examination, Christian's demeanor was warm and friendly, and he seemed to enjoy his cordial exchange with Johnnie Cochran. And after almost every question, he looked over at O.J. as if to say, "I gave the right answer, didn't I?"

However, the minute the prosecution took over, a drastic personality change occurred. Christian became arrogant and somewhat obstinate. He seemed willing to say anything to protect his friend and himself. When, to show Christian's financial ties to O.J., prosecutor Christopher Darden asked if O.J. had planned to finance the production of some exercise equipment he and O.J. had been working on, Christian's answer was no even though he was working with the manufacturer in Culver City whom I had found, Earl Trusty at Farrufino's. Earl had made the prototype for Christian, and Christian had told him that O.J. would be financing the project. Christian did not have that kind of money, so if O.J. hadn't planned to finance it, there is no way he could have undertaken the project.

Even more incredibly, Christian had become so vicious that he could actually suggest that Nicole deserved to die and then deny it under oath. When Darden asked Christian if he had said that Nicole deserved to have her throat slit, Christian said no. For once he told the truth—he did not use those exact words. What he actually said to Candace and me was, "All three of them—Nicole, Cora, and Faye—got exactly what they deserved. They neglected their children by going out at night and separating themselves from O.J., Ron, and me."

Even if Christian's statement about us were true, since when is going dancing a capital offense punishable by death? For a person even to think in such terms is horrible. Further, he is a chiropractor who should uphold the value of human life. It was very painful for me to realize that this man I had held so close to my heart, who had portrayed himself as a person of integrity and spirituality, had gone so completely astray.

When Darden asked Christian if O.J. had been depressed about Nicole leaving him, Christian said no, but when Darden pursued that line of questioning and reminded him of his original statement to the investigators, Christian was forced to answer more truthfully. Although he would not acknowledge the simple, well-known fact that Nicole had left O.J., he admitted that O.J. had been depressed and angry about the fact that their relationship did not work out.

He also said it was a mutual parting of ways. If that were true, why did Nicole throw a diamond-and-sapphire bracelet along with a pair of diamond earrings in O.J.'s face one week before the murder? She told him, "Get away from me and stay out of my life. I cannot be bought, and I want nothing more to do with you." That was another slap in O.J.'s face and a further indication that Nicole was truly through with him. He was furious! Christian knew that, but when Darden asked him about it he softened it by saying that Nicole had simply given them back.

Then, when Darden asked Christian if he knew what had happened to that jewelry, Christian said no. He was lying. He knew that within days O.J. had given both the bracelet and the earrings to Paula Barbieri, the lady he supposedly was not seeing anymore.

Christian and O.J. had countless conversations about how upset O.J. was that Nicole was leaving him. But when he was asked about their separation, Christian said it was "a mutual decision." That was so far from the truth that I was shocked.

One of Christian's most outrageous statements was when Christopher Darden asked him if he had ever considered writing a book about Nicole. He said he had not, but that he had talked about writing a book on ethics. What does this man know of ethics? Maybe the book would be about the *lack* of ethics. That would be more believable. What Darden was referring to was *Private Diary*, which Christian had wanted to write with me.

Even though I promised myself I would never talk to him again, when Christian finished testifying I could not resist leaving one final message on his machine. I told him that he had betrayed not only Nicole, but also himself, and he would someday have to answer to God.

Chapter 9

BLAMING FAYE

LOS ANGELES, CALIFORNIA
NOVEMBER–DECEMBER 1994

After I returned to California, it was decided by my publisher that I should do interviews with certain people. Jeffrey Toobin, who writes for *The New Yorker*, was one of them. Although Toobin was the journalist who first put out the story that Mark Fuhrman may have planted the glove, I didn't know that when we met for the interview at the Century Plaza Hotel. While I tried to be pleasant, Toobin seemed strange—almost paranoid. It wasn't long before I began to understand why. His article, called "Blaming Faye," described me as someone who had "dabbled in charity projects and worked hard on her appearance." He included the defense team's Colombian drug cartel ploys and laid out a scenario for them. Throughout, he implied that there was no validity to anything I had said or written. I have always admired and respected *The New Yorker*, but— needless to say—I was disappointed in the shallowness of Toobin's article.

A little later I had an interview with *People* magazine that was also quite peculiar. *People* sent a questionnaire asking me to dictate the answers on tape. They interviewed my ex-husband, Paul Resnick, for two solid hours and used exactly one paragraph. Paul, one of my very dearest friends, called me after the interview and said, "Faye, I had a lot of very good things to say about you. In fact, that was ninety-nine percent of the interview." Paul was furious when the article appeared. Instead of using the positive things he had said, they chose to twist his statements around so he sounded negative. It was insane, but I quickly realized that few journalists and few publications have any desire to report the truth because the truth doesn't sell.

Though *People* had assured us that they would do a balanced piece, it was anything but balanced. Their authority was a person named Peter, who supposedly was hired as a sort of public relations man by "friends of Nicole." Not one of us had ever heard of him. He had just dug up all the misinformation that had ever been printed and that's what *People* used in their article. It was cruel and destructive, and it was obviously planned to discredit me and everything I was doing.

Almost a year later there were two other interviews that were especially disappointing: one was with "Entertainment Tonight" and the other was with a similar show, "Extra." I agreed to do them because it was near the anniversary of Nicole's death and I felt it was important to keep Nicole and the domestic violence issue in the public eye.

"Extra" was not interested in honoring Nicole— they were merely after the sensational. They played an excerpt from the audio of *Private Diary* that was totally irrelevant to the occasion. Then they said, "Is Faye Resnick a profiteer or is she a voice of honesty?" I think that they knew the answer, but they chose to disregard it.

Months later I met the managing editor of *People* magazine, Landon "Lanny" Jones, Jr. I sat next to him at dinner at Drai's. Lanny turned to me and said the same thing David Margolick had said in Vermont: "You are nothing like I imagined you would be."

I said, "Well, the press has created this monster. They have portrayed me as something I'm not, so why would you or anyone else expect me to be any different?"

Right after the dinner was over, he said, "I'd love to do a piece on you."

I could only say, "Lanny, you must be crazy!"

He looked puzzled. "Why is that?"

"Because your magazine did a completely vicious piece on me. It belittled me and the constructive things I am trying to do. You used information from a man none of Nicole's friends had ever heard of and told your readers that he was hired by one of us. It really looked as if it had been set up by someone on the payroll of the defense."

He seemed truly sorry. "I cannot believe that they did not give you a balanced piece."

I said, "Lanny, that's what happened."

The next thing he did was ask me to go with him to another table to meet the president of *People* and one of the producers of "Extra."

"I hope you don't mind that I dragged you over here to meet my friends," he said later.

I could only say, "I find it interesting that after these people have slammed me, I am expected to be gracious to them and to act as if it is just a game. Well, since you asked, I'll answer you. The reality is, it is not just a game—it's my life. And everything that is said about me affects my child."

The producer of "Extra" said he considered what they had done "a nice piece." I politely told him that I considered it a kill job. When they said they were really sorry, I replied, "I have always believed that we can try to correct our mistakes."

When we got back to our table, Lanny said, "How could you have sat here during the entire dinner and been so pleasant to me?"

I said, "I choose not to be rude. There is nothing you can do about that story now. It has already run and I'm sure it wasn't something that you personally intended to do to me. I gather that in Media 101 they teach you that the individual you are writing about is not a real person, so you shouldn't worry too much about the facts and never worry about how anyone feels. Just write whatever will sell."

He was very apologetic, but the fact remains that the *People* magazine piece was just horrible. Little did I know that there would be others that were even worse. Soon after *Private Diary* came out, I learned that in addition to attacking the book and my credibility, the media would also take other cheap shots. "A Current Affair" led the parade. They interviewed a woman they described as a "close friend of the Resnick family." I had never heard of her and nobody I spoke with in the Resnick family had ever met her. She turned out to be one of the "Current Affair" reporters.

She explained how poor I had become—that I used to drive a Rolls-Royce, but I was cut off and now had to drive a Mercedes. She also said that I had lived in a mansion in Beverly Hills, spent a fortune, and then tried to push myself to the front of the Beverly Hills social circle.

But it got much nastier than that. They displayed a copy of what they claimed were my records from the Betty Ford Center. After showing the forged records, "Current Affair" went on to say, "How could anyone believe this woman who has been in drug treatment and has admitted to having blackouts?"

But they did not stop there. "Current Affair" interviewed my stepdaughter Jackie, one of Paul Resnick's daughters, and did an especially cruel piece called "Stepmommy Dearest."

Then there was *Raging Heart*, whose author, Sheila Weller, talked about how, with my Chanel suits and my charity work, I had pushed myself to the forefront of Beverly Hills society. And then, after making it seem as if that were my only identity, she went on to say that I had been so determined to get out the vote in a local election that I had gone on working when I had a temperature of 103 degrees.

What was her point? Was it that I just wanted to have my name in the papers or that I was so committed to helping others that I would go on working even when I was very ill? At least that part was accurate. It was during the campaign of a friend, Jo Anne Kopland, who was seeking a seat on the Beverly Hills Board of Education. I knew she would be excellent and I wanted her to win. I had just come back from Mexico where I had picked up a bug. I felt dreadful, but I was not willing to stop working. The candidate my friend was running against had run before and was very well known, so Jo Anne's chances of winning were slim. I did everything I could to get the vote out and to get her elected. She won and not only did she go on to do an incredible job, she is now vice president of the Board of Education.

Sheila Weller paid the Browns $100,000 to get their input on her book about Nicole. Then word went around that the Browns had a dispute with her because they did not like what she had written. Neither did I.

She described our group in great detail. She interviewed everyone except me because while she was writing her book, I was writing mine. The portrait of the others came out the way they wanted them. But that is often the case—if you give writers the information they want, they may be kind to you. If you don't or if they don't know you, they feel free to write what they please.

Weller described me as a character out of a Judith Krantz novel and said I was the most exotic of the group. It was as if she did not quite know what to say about me, so she contradicted herself, speaking very highly of me and criticizing me at the same time. Had she interviewed me, it may have gone differently.

Among other things, she questioned my racial background. For the record, I am Italian, Spanish, and English, or—to be more precise—I am Corsican, Castilian, and Anglo-Saxon. But I stay very tan and that may give some people the impression that I am black. I am not. If I were, I would gladly say so. That's a trivial detail, mentioned only to show her uninformed approach.

* * *

Around Thanksgiving, my second interview with David Margolick came out and he reported that I had been telling the truth all along. Others were learning that, too.

The Brown family had found Nicole's diary in her safety deposit box and turned it over to the prosecution. Nicole had documented the abuse, describing exactly what had happened during the years she was with O.J. The jury was permitted to hear about only a few of the incidents because it was considered hearsay, but the media and the public heard it all. Suddenly reporters were calling asking to interview me, saying that they had not believed me but now knew I'd been right all along.

Associated Press ran a story saying that I had now been vindicated. One journalist asked me how I felt about that. My answer was that I had not needed vindication—I had always known that what I said was true. I was just glad that the public would now know that O.J. was an abuser and that his rage was a clear motive for murder.

I was distressed that Nicole had documented something like sixty-one incidents and the jurors were able to hear about so few. Nicole's premonition that she was going to be killed clearly revealed by the papers, articles, and clippings in her safety deposit box. It was obvious that she was convinced that O.J. was going to murder her and that she wanted the world to know exactly what he had done.

About a month before the murders O.J. called me in a tantrum about something—this happened so often that I can't remember what it was about that time—and again he told me that he would kill Nicole. I could hear that he was getting more desperate and I tried to convince Nicole to protect herself. I begged her, "Nic, you really need to write this down, see an attorney, and go to the police. We can't let this happen." She promised me that it was all in her diary and I had to take her word for it. Even so, O.J. seemed so out of control, I worried about her practically around the clock.

Nicole could be inflexible. The last time I urged her to get away from O.J., she said, "I am staying here and that's all there is to it. I understand that you might not agree, Faye, but at this point I'm not asking for your opinion or advice. Because you're my friend I confide in you, but you have to let me do things my own way."

Of course I respected her request, but I wanted to bring the whole situation out in the open—I felt that if we exposed it, Nicole would be safe. But she was convinced that if she did anything to hurt his image, O.J. definitely would kill her.

Chapter 10

BOOK TOUR AND BEYOND

USA, CANADA, AND ENGLAND
DECEMBER 1994–AUGUST 1995

*A*lthough my book tour was a very short three-stop stint over a period of just a few weeks, considering what had gone on after the publication of *Private Diary,* it was no less daunting. When I was first told I was scheduled to do a book signing at Brentano's at the Beverly Center in Los Angeles, I was apprehensive because I had been so publicly criticized. I was also frightened that if my whereabouts became public, someone might try to harm me. Because I was assured security would be tight, I agreed to go through with it. I didn't have any idea of what to expect, so that evening when I walked into the store, I was astonished at the chaos. It was media madness—I had never seen anything like it. On one side of the store, there were five security guards along with CNN, "Hard Copy," print journalists, photographers, and local and network news crews. On the other side of the store, people were standing in line waiting to have their books signed. So many flashbulbs, lights, and cameras were in my face that I couldn't see what I was writing. I felt as if I were under a microscope. It was unbelievable!

Even though my publicist had told the media that we wouldn't be making any comments, reporters kept asking questions about how I felt about testifying. Finally I told them that, though I had volunteered to be a prosecution witness, I was not looking forward to the trial, testifying, or any of the other things that I felt I had to do as a result of Nicole's murder. The questions kept flying, yet through all the noise, I could hear a woman with a soft voice asking intelligent, sensitive questions about Nicole and the case. I couldn't actually see her in the crowd, but I remembered her voice and was impressed that she was not seeking the sensational quotes the others were after.

I had committed to be there for an hour, and by the time I looked up, I had signed fifty or more books and had just enough time to catch a glimpse of two women walking into the store. "How does she know O.J. beat Nicole—was she there?" one asked the other at the top of her lungs. "I read her book and she's just out to get O.J. and trying to make money on her friend's death." It was a nightmare! Fortunately, by the time the security guard escorted these people out, the book signing was over. Because of the media circus and the hecklers, I left as soon as I could, missing some friends I had worked with on various charities and campaigns who had to come to surprise me. They arrived five minutes after I had left, and were inundated by reporters asking, "Isn't it typical of Faye Resnick not to be there for her friends?" They quickly defended me and tried to talk about how great I was and all the fine things I had done. Guess what? The TV cameras were turned off. The press did not want to hear any good things about Faye Resnick.

As we were walking out of Brentano's, I mentioned the female reporter in the audience to my publicist Warren Cowan. "I would like to give her an interview. I'm not sure, but I think she had light hair and she had a camera crew with her. She asked very sensitive questions. They were about Nicole, but also about domestic violence. I'd like to know who she is."

One of Warren's assistants returned to find her and brought back her card. "You're not going to believe this," Warren said. "She's from 'Hard Copy.'" That was unexpected, because "Hard Copy" is not known for its sensitivity or soft-spoken reporters. It is one of the most professional of all the TV tabloids, but it is still a tabloid. I thought, *I would really love to speak with her, no matter where she is from.*

Around the time of the Brentano's book signing in December, the press started asking for more interviews. They now realized that the book told the truth and that I had something serious to say about what was going on. They also understood that I had provided valuable information to the prosecution. One person I met during this period was Vincent Bugliosi, the brilliant former Los Angeles prosecutor who said he thought the information was invaluable. "If I were a prosecutor and had the information that you turned over, I would consider it a road map to exactly what happened," he said. "You could never ask for more from a witness, and even if you are never on the witness stand, you have given them everything they could ever want."

As it turned out, the prosecution decided not to call me as a witness because the drug issue lowered my credibility. To me, that was ridiculous. It is true that I have lived a very full, colorful, and sometimes unconventional life, but it didn't mean that I was lacking integrity. To suggest that people shouldn't believe anyone who has ever had a problem with drugs or alcohol would be eliminating millions of the good citizens of this country. But, as we know, bright and devious attorneys can turn almost anything into whatever they want it to be.

Throughout this ordeal of being attacked by the press, I was grateful for reporters who had the courage to support me. One was syndicated columnist Liz Smith, who had written a column that challenged the various judgments that were being thrown around about my credibility. "How unfortunate that people won't believe Faye Resnick because she did drugs," Smith wrote. "It's as if she's the only one on the planet." I had not yet met her at that point, but I certainly admired her for standing her ground when it was clearly not a popular position to take.

When we did eventually meet for lunch a few weeks after the column was published, not only did she want to know about the book and about Nicole and O.J., but was also interested in what I was trying to do for women who were victims of abuse. In the sea of people who had blatant disregard for my message, I was grateful for Liz Smith's support.

* * *

A few weeks before the book tour began, I was able to find some time to relax. I went to visit my sister in Marin County and finally get a few things out of storage. It had been months since I had seen and worn some of my things and I was finally beginning to feel like myself again.

The first leg of the book tour was Canada. When I arrived, accompanied by my friend CiCi Shahian, we were met by a representative of General Publishing, the Canadian publisher of *Private Diary*. Thankfully the Canadian media were both sensitive and serious about the domestic violence aspect of the book. I was scheduled to do about twenty-five interviews—television, radio, and a lot of print—throughout my five days in Canada.

As soon as I arrived, I asked the publisher to obtain some statistics for me on domestic violence in Canada, hoping to gain an understanding of the situation there. Regardless of how I am treated, I regard interviews as opportunities to air my campaign against domestic violence. The interviewers always want to talk about scandal, so I give them a little scandal and then talk about the issue most important to me: domestic violence. The members of the press have to listen to what I have to say whether they want to or not. This is why I try to do live shows whenever possible because they can't edit out what I have to say.

Three days after I arrived in Canada, the government started a major TV campaign on domestic violence. I don't know how it began, and though I doubt that I had anything to do with it, it was a happy coincidence. I was delighted to find a nation that took this problem seriously, and the fact is Canadians have worked hard on the problem of domestic violence. For example, even if a woman will not testify against her husband, when there has been an emergency call and they see that the woman has been battered, the government takes legal action.

People may think that book tours are very glamorous and authors just spend their time gallivanting around to museums, the opera, the theater, and great restaurants, but that is not the case. The schedule was so packed, neither CiCi nor I had time to take a deep breath. By the end of each day I was totally exhausted because throughout this time, in addition to being "on" for days at a time, I was also reliving Nicole's death and the aftermath. In some cultures they believe that if someone takes your photograph without your permission, part of your spirit is taken, too. That's how it felt to me doing so many interviews each day. I was physically and emotionally drained and needed my evenings to recover. After interviews, CiCi and I usually returned to the hotel to relax and eat dinner in our room.

But of course, that fact did not stop the *Star*, which announced that I was buying luxury items at Chanel and Tiffany's, from giving the impression we spent our time running around on some mad shopping spree. The fact is I bought a hat because it was freezing and my ears were cold. Nevertheless, Michael Viner faxed the article to me with a playful note saying, "If we gave you time to shop, we should have booked more interviews." I called Dove's offices and relayed the message that if I had to do one more interview, it would have had to have been while I was in the bathtub.

I also did a book signing in Canada. Unlike book signings in the United States, they invite authors to come in and autograph their books, but they don't have people lined up to buy them. After I had signed about a hundred books, they gave me a tour of the store. Every book you could ever want to read was there—I was in awe of the enormous amount of creativity under one roof

The next stop was London, where Penguin had published a paperback edition of *Private Diary*. I was distressed to see the cover, which included a photograph of O.J. and Nicole together, but Penguin explained that British readers would not recognize Nicole by herself. While the Penguin representatives were extremely gracious, I had lived in London for a year—Francesca was born there—and I was familiar with the tabloid tactics of the London press and knew what to expect. Needless to say, I was not looking forward to what came next.

My first interview there was on "UK Living," their biggest morning show. As I walked on the set, the hosts were speaking, via satellite, with a British correspondent who was covering the O.J. Simpson trial in Los Angeles. The moment they introduced me, the reporter began a campaign to discredit me. "Even though Faye Resnick has written a book," she announced matter-of-factly, "you shouldn't believe anything she says. She takes drugs and they think she had something to do with the murders." By the time she had finished, she had called me a profiteer and made several other insulting remarks.

I could only say, "First of all, I would like to make it clear that there is no truth to what she said. I did not write *Private Diary* just to make money. This book is about domestic violence. It's about seeing a relationship unfold, knowing how it would end, and being unable to stop it from happening. It has been authenticated by three reliable sources and, regardless of what your correspondent may believe, everything in it is completely accurate."

The host cut me off with, "Thank you very much, Faye Resnick." And that was the end of it. I thought, *No wonder people complain about the arrogance of the Brits.*

The following day I did a morning talk show in Manchester. There were two hosts—a husband-and-wife team. When we went on the air, the man seemed hostile and determined to attack me. Like others, he accused me of trying to make money from Nicole's death, putting too much sex in the book, and anything else negative that he could think of. It was not an interview but a series of attacks. His wife wanted to be fair and tried to calm him down, but there was no stopping him. I finally said, "Pardon me, but I did not come here to be abused. I came here to tell a story that has very serious implications." And he stopped. I'm sure that he would have preferred not to air that interview, but it was live so there was nothing he could do about it.

I guess I got my point across because as I left, people in the studio came up to me saying, "We cannot believe he attacked you that way," "He refuses to enter the twentieth century," and "Thank you for putting him in his place."

In England I did thirty television and radio interviews and met with a number of print journalists. There were some good radio interviews, and a couple of them were wonderful. Many women and even a few men were very interested in what I had to say.

The only time I had ever been attacked on a live show before my England tour was on Maury Povich, but there I was attacked by the audience, not by the host, and I had since learned a lot about giving interviews. I knew I had to defend myself quickly, and be brief and concise so that there was no space for them to edit out what I said. Although I was shocked by how aggressive some of the British media people could be, I was able to cope because I had grown accustomed to hostile journalists over the past few months.

When I got back to Los Angeles, the friends I had worked with on my charity projects, many of whom had children who went to school with Francesca, came to see me or called me. Every one of them told me she was behind me. I will always remember what one said: "We are your champions. We will never let anyone say anything bad about you because we know the truth." That was a very important validation, because I had started wondering if I was just imagining that I had been a solid and constructive person in the past. That's how much the negative publicity had been able to infiltrate my sanity.

Little did I know what was to come next. "Hard Copy" contacted me and asked if I would be interested in being a commentator on the trial. At first I was ambivalent, but then I remembered the reporter's soft voice at Brentano's and decided it was an opportunity to get some true facts before the public.

I agreed to do ten segments commenting on the trial as it progressed. At a time when so much misinformation was being put out, I regarded it as an opportunity to give viewers a reality check. It was a big-audience show, with 175 affiliate stations, so I was able to get my message out to a large number of people.

"Hard Copy" was an interesting experience even though I was less than thrilled that my commentary was crunched between the celebrity scandals of the month. We did the ten segments over a one-month period during which I commented on the testimony of Denise Brown, Cynthia Shahian, and Candace Garvey. The show was also interested in exploring some of the things that had been cut out of the original version of *Private Diary*. (At the last minute close to 10,000 words were cut from the original manuscript.) When asked about Nicole's notes from her safety deposit box that the defense kept the jury from seeing, I could barely contain myself.

"Those are words from the grave," I said. "That's Nicole speaking. How could they suppress evidence like that? If they were convinced that O.J. Simpson was really innocent, they would want all the evidence to come out."

At about the same time, I was also looking for a new home for Francesca and me. Francesca was at her father's and I was staying at a friend's condominium in Century City. Upon my return from a house-hunting expedition one afternoon, I received a call from Dove telling me that I was scheduled to be on "Larry King Live" that evening, leaving me less than two hours to get dressed and travel across town during rush hour. We were scheduled to go on at exactly five o'clock, and at four fifty-five I was stuck in traffic on Sunset Boulevard. I called from my car phone and said, "If you will have someone waiting out front to take my car, I'll dash to the studio and definitely be there on time."

When I pulled into the CNN lot, I threw my key to the first person I saw and rushed into the elevator. As the door opened, someone grabbed my arm, threw me into Larry King's guest seat, and at that instant the cameras started rolling.

Contrary to my expectations, although he was Larry King—fast as usual—he was kind, and the interview was not only informative but also enjoyable. Larry does a fine job of balancing interesting stories with hard news without being a scandal monger.

Of all the interviews, there was one that I especially appreciated—with O.J. trial commentator Kathleen Sullivan on "E!" She had attended USC with O.J. and had fond memories of those days, yet didn't lose her perspective. She opened the interview by saying, "I'm so pleased to meet you—I respect you very much. You have been the voice of truth that Nicole needed, and I thank you for that." What impressed me was that she focused on women's issues and domestic violence, asking me about the trial and all that had happened in the year since Nicole's death. She aired about forty-five minutes of our interview and I felt it was a loving tribute to Nicole.

Rosie Grier was also on the same program. You couldn't have asked for a more balanced show—I was there for Nicole and Grier was there for O.J. He is a minister and had been visiting O.J. in jail. His position, of course, was that O.J. was innocent.

Rosie is a very decent person, and may very well know that O.J. killed Nicole. At the trial, the prosecution attempted to offer evidence that a deputy overheard O.J. admit to Rosie that O.J. did in fact commit the murders. However, because any such communication was viewed by Judge Ito as a communication between a minister and his penitent, Judge Ito ruled that the law protects that communication from disclosure and that even if the deputy did overhear such a statement, it could not be used in the trial.

In the same week Kathleen Sullivan did a special on domestic violence, interviewing a woman from a shelter. She really did her part to remember the anniversary of Nicole's death. I have met many credible journalists, and she's one of them.

Robert Vito is another. He works in the Los Angeles Bureau of CNN and, like David Margolick, is fair, balanced, and extremely sensitive. During my interview with him, he asked some very tough questions, but always gave me a chance to reply. And he didn't edit my responses. You see, in a taped interview, you never know what they are going to edit out—you can answer a question one way and they can edit it to make it sound totally different. Robert did not. He made his points and he let me make mine.

Later we did a special interview around the anniversary of Nicole's death and discussed my research for *Shattered,* which I was preparing to write. He drove home a point that had been becoming clearer to me. He said, "You know, Faye, you came out and told the truth before the media or the public were ready to confront it. The more you insisted that the facts be examined, the more threatening you became. And people respond to threats with hostility."

I now know that if you are willing to tell an unpopular truth, you have to be willing to be attacked—and willing to become unpopular yourself.

PART III

The Liars Club

*Every violation of truth is not only
a sort of suicide in the liar,
but is a stab at the health
of human society.*

—Emerson

Men lie, who lack courage to tell the truth.

—Joaquin Miller

Chapter 11

THE CREATIVE O.J.

*T*he O.J. Simpson trial was basically one long lie, and the number one liar was O.J. Simpson himself. The day that he said, "Absolutely one hundred percent not guilty," Nicole's friends could not believe those words could come rolling off his tongue. But he's an actor, and he was giving his best performance ever. Whether you have ever been around O.J. or not, you could see that he was more concerned about the damage to his image than the murder of the mother of his children. His arrogant attitude seemed to suggest that the trial was a trivial formality and an imposition on his time.

When the defense claimed that O.J. was too arthritic to commit such a crime, I wanted to say, "If he was so arthritic, how could he be punching the numbers on a cellular phone? And why would he be using a cellular phone right outside of his house— why wouldn't he take his portable phone outside instead of paying the cellular charge? And where was he hitting the golf balls—in Justin's sandbox in the dark?" That did not make sense to me, either, because the sandbox was in the backyard. Anyway, there was no room in the sandbox to hit a golf ball, so he would have had to have been in the front yard because that's where the limousine driver saw a black man walk toward the door.

When O.J. was questioned about why he had a disguise with him, he said that he had taken his children to Disneyland a couple of weeks ago and he did not want to be noticed. I have been to Disneyland with the Simpsons and he did not wear a disguise—he loved the attention. In fact, everywhere he went, O.J. wanted to be noticed, and if he was not he would raise his voice level to make sure that everyone around knew that O.J. Simpson was there. When he wasn't noticed, his mood would change and he would become angry or depressed.

O.J. was all about power and he always had to feel that he was in control and the center of attention. He hated to go to Europe because nobody there knew who he was. He said to Nicole,

"I didn't work my entire life to build my image and reputation to go places where they don't recognize and respect me." So we can be sure that a visit to Disneyland was not the reason that he had the disguise in the Bronco.

The lies went on from there. O.J. said that he had parked one of his other cars on Rockingham, but he never parked his Bronco there. O.J. had to park on Rockingham that night because the limousine driver was at the Ashley entrance and would have seen him pull up. Also, the Bronco was parked at an angle, sticking out into the street. O.J. said he parked that way because he was in a hurry. Why? He had time to go home, play golf, sleep, and do all the other things he claimed he had been doing.

Also puzzling are the reports that O.J. almost missed the plane to Chicago. That's more significant than it sounds. One of his pet peeves was being late. The many times I traveled with O.J. and Nicole, he always made a big point of being early. That makes it even more strange that he would have stopped to take a nap and hit golf balls when he knew the limousine would be there. And why did he take the time to make phone calls on his cellular phone while he was outside his own front door? O.J. could have made those calls on the way to the airport in the limousine.

O.J. is a very meticulous man. Everything in his life had to be perfectly organized, and he was obsessive about neatness. No one ever saw O.J.'s car parked at an angle before. It was always very carefully placed, as was his wardrobe, as was everything in his house. He was so fanatic that Nicole told me he once beat her because she did not line up the towels perfectly in his bathroom. That's how he was about neatness. Nothing could ever be one inch out of place.

When I asked Nicole how O.J. could have beat her for such an insignificant thing, she said, "Because O.J. had told me over and over again that his towels had to be placed exactly the way he had told me." That was after he had put a brass "No Smoking" plaque in the bathroom because that's where she used to sneak her cigarettes.

After the divorce I went to Nicole's house once and it was a real mess. I said, "What's going on, Nic? Your house used to be so neat!" And she said, "I have bad feelings about keeping my house in perfect order. O.J. made neatness such a high priority, and I don't want to live like that any longer. I'm enjoying having my house feel comfortable and lived in. I feel that it's a home now.

"My children could never play in our house before because they might mess it up. I tried to explain to O.J. that it was okay for kids to do that, but he insisted that they be confined to the upstairs playroom, and that was the only place in our house where they could have their toys.

"Even when we would be outside in the pool area, the toys had to be arranged properly. Everything had to be in its precise place, otherwise O.J. would throw a tantrum. And if he happened to be in a bad mood, it could end up as a disaster for me."

That's why the story about the car parked at an angle did not sound even remotely possible. That's just not something O.J. Simpson would allow himself to do, especially when he was leaving for a trip.

When Detectives Vannatter and Lange told O.J. that blood had been found at his house, he explained that he had mysteriously cut himself before he took off for Chicago. However, his then-good friend, police officer Ron Shipp, who was with O.J. the night he returned from Chicago, testified that O.J. asked him how long it takes to get the results of DNA tests and confided that he didn't want to take a lie detector test because he had had dreams of killing Nicole.

Shipp also testified that he would sometimes bring some of his friends on the police force to the

Rockingham estate to show them around and meet O.J. He said O.J. always welcomed them and they thought O.J. was the greatest. It doesn't make sense that these people would turn around and enter into a conspiracy against their hero.

At one point Shipp was asked why he would say anything that might be damaging to his friend O.J. Simpson. Shipp looked directly at O.J. and said that he couldn't stand to have Nicole's blood on his conscience. The defense went after him, of course, and attacked his credibility by bringing up his past problems with alcohol. They also ridiculed him for having told anyone about O.J.'s dream and continued with their intimidation tactics by implying that he had been with women at O.J.'s estate.

As I saw Shipp's distress at having to reveal facts that might hurt O.J., and then watched the defense tearing away at him, I knew how he must have felt. The last thing in the world that either of us could ever have imagined was happening. A man we had both loved and respected not only had killed our friend Nicole but also was now masterminding attacks on us.

The defense team eventually offered a $500,000 reward to anyone who could provide information leading to the killer. They knew full well they would never have to pay up because they knew exactly who killed Nicole and Ron—they were defending him.

Many thought that for that kind of money there were people in this country who would turn in their own brothers, even if they knew they had not committed the crime. But to the amazement of the defense, no one came forward. I've often wondered why they didn't offer the reward immediately after the murders. Perhaps it took them a while to remember that they had to at least *pretend* that the murderer was still at large. I guess even the Dream Team made mistakes once in a while.

What amazed me was the way all of the brilliant legal experts who had analyzed this case from every angle could have overlooked such common-sense errors. My question is, what case are they analyzing? Vincent Bugliosi was one of the first lawyers with the courage to step forward and say for the record that O.J. Simpson was guilty in a long interview in the December 1994 issue of *Playboy* magazine. Vincent spent eight years as a prosecutor for the Los Angeles District Attorney's office—during which time he tried close to 1,000 cases, including the Manson family murder trial—and went on to become an award-winning author.

He said that the O.J. Simpson trial is sensational for only one reason: O.J. Simpson. "When you remove him from the equation, this is not an unusual murder case. He obviously killed his former wife and her male companion out of passion and rage. . . ." He also said, "In all my years in criminal law, other than cases in which the killer has been apprehended during the perpetration of the homicide, I've never seen such an obvious case of guilt."

I don't have many heroes in this world but Vincent Bugliosi will always be one of mine. I feel honored that I have come to know him and his wife, who both exude honesty and integrity.

* * *

For months I have been struggling for an understanding that would allow the forgiveness that I can't find in my heart. It became very clear to me that O.J. has been a fighter all of his life. As a child, he had to develop strong survival instincts. After he recovered from the rickets his playmates teased him about when he was very young, he swore he would never be ridiculed again. He became a bully and a thug. Growing up in Potrero Hills, a then-rough section of San Francisco, he faced a world full of poverty, bigotry, and obstacles. He once told me how difficult it was for him and that he would always do anything to get over it. He went on to say that he had learned certain lessons early in his life. One was to deny, deny, deny. He explained that if you deny something long enough and come up with a good enough story, people will begin to believe you.

We had this conversation during our last trip to Cabo San Lucas. I had asked O.J. how he had become so successful and how he was able to get away with constantly cheating on Nicole. (The sad fact is that he was equally proud of both.) Of course, he quickly added that the cheating was a thing of the past—that once they reconciled he never would think of cheating again.

That was an outright lie. O.J. continued to see Paula Barbieri throughout his attempt to reconcile with Nicole. He denied it, but he could no longer fool Nicole. That was one of the things that finally freed her from his spell, and he knew it!

About a month later, when O.J. could feel Nicole pulling further away, he told me, "Nicole left me once before and even though I didn't like it, I let her go. But to do this to me again after begging me to come back. . . . I will not let her publicly humiliate me for a second time. I know she must be seeing someone else. If I find out she is with another man, I'll kill her. I will kill that bitch!"

When she let him know that she could not go through with the reconciliation and that she wanted nothing further to do with him, he couldn't stand the thought that she would humiliate him again. Then, at Sydney's dance recital just hours before the murders, she told O.J. in front of others that they really were finished and he was not to consider himself a part of her family any longer. That was when she signed her death sentence.

* * *

I was physically ill for two days after I read the description of the viewing of photographs of the murder scene in the book that dismissed juror Michael Knox wrote with Mike Walker. And I feel sick every time I think of it.

"Family members sobbed, turned away, or reacted somehow," Knox wrote. "But inevitably everyone forced themselves to look. Except O.J. Simpson. He never looked at the mutilated bodies of his ex-wife and Ron Goldman.

"It was far gorier than I had expected. Yet I felt relieved in one respect: You could not see that Nicole's head had been nearly severed from her body. Thankfully, her hair covered that awful wound, but it was still horrible. Nicole was lying in blood that pooled out from her head and flowed down along her body. Such a huge amount of blood. It had drained down the condo walkway. Yet Nicole looked so still, almost peaceful, that if it weren't for the blood, you would have thought she was lying on her side asleep in her black halter dress. I looked across the courtroom at O.J. I'd been intent on the pictures, but I glanced at him several times. He still had not looked at his dead ex-wife."

O.J. could afford to buy the best. His defense team—a collection of high-priced, high-profile lawyers—seemed prepared to stop at nothing to absolve their client of any blame for these murders. I realize that defense lawyers are paid to defend their clients, but it is my understanding that they are supposed to have certain standards of ethics. Because of the outright, outrageous, totally unfounded lies they have concocted about me, I cannot help questioning the truth of other things they have said.

When he was being interviewed for an article, Bugliosi explained, "One canon of ethics of the American Bar Association provides that a 'lawyer should represent a client zealously,'" but adds, "'within the bounds of the law.'"

O.J.'s lawyers seemed involved in a battle that went beyond this case. I don't know if it was because they were embarrassed by their tactics, trying to bolster their egos, or striving to save their reputations. We have to consider the influence of the defendant. O.J. Simpson has always believed that he and he alone should call the shots for everyone and everything around him. And he has always known how to dominate others and use his charm and his strength to manipulate the truth and the system. Maybe that is what he did with his lawyers.

I know it may be hard to believe, but I think O.J. was actually enjoying the whole procedure. He is so egocentric that he loves being at center stage of world. As he sat there, arrogant and smirking, it was clear that this was not a man grieving for the loss of his beautiful ex-wife, the mother of his children.

In his book, O.J. said that the key to the death of Nicole and Ron could be found in the drug world that Faye Resnick inhabited. He knows full well that's a lie. The truth is he sees the key to the death of Nicole and Ron every time he looks in the mirror.

Chapter 12

MORE LIES AND LIARS

JOHNNIE COCHRAN

When Johnnie Cochran decided that O.J. Simpson would not be testifying, it seemed he took over telling O.J.'s lies. In his opening statement, he said, "Let's talk about Nicole Simpson's friend Faye Resnick." He made five allegations about me. The only one that had any truth to it was that I had used drugs. Although he greatly exaggerated the amount I had used, it was true that I had used drugs and I had never denied it. But everything else was a fabrication invented by him or O.J.

He described Nicole and me as party girls who had to go out three or four times every week. That is not true. We both had children and they were our first priority. Depending on our schedules and theirs, we went out sometimes once a week or even once a month. And we usually went out with Christian and O.J. So, that was another of his many distortions of the truth.

Cochran's contention that I had no place to live because Christian Reichardt threw me out of his house was another lie. I was never thrown out of Christian's house. I left there because I needed a break from Christian, so I went to stay at my friend Kathy's house and then I went to stay with Nicole and her kids for a few days, which is the way many women handle the situation when they are having problems with their mates.

He suggested that I had been thrown out of the house because my drug use was so extreme that Christian could no longer tolerate it. The fact is, Christian didn't have any idea that I was using drugs until Nicole called him the day before I went into Exodus and said, "Faye is using drugs and I feel that she needs to go into treatment." I had relapsed and had been using drugs for about two weeks, and only a very small amount. Because my system just can't handle them, the quantity of drugs that I have ever used was very minimal.

The "expensive drug use" that Johnnie Cochran described was in reality costing me between $20 and $30 dollars a day. It's easy to get drugs in such small amounts. I was getting mine from a friend who was not part of our circle. He was a recreational drug user and whenever I wanted any I got them from him. There was no question of whether I could afford the few dollars they cost. I paid him cash every single time.

One of Cochran's most outrageous statements was that Christian had refused to give me money for drugs. I never asked Christian for money for anything and I certainly never asked him for money for drugs. Moreover, Christian didn't have any money to give me—I was giving *him* money. I had more than $20,000 in my safety deposit box, I had money in the bank, and because Christian was going through my money so quickly, I had asked my sister Patsy to hold some funds for me. Christian always wanted money for something— he had just talked me into lending twenty thousand dollars to one of his friends. I didn't know what he was going to think of next so I did not want to have too much money around.

Cochran stated as fact, "Faye Resnick used drugs right after she had her breast implants." That was half true. I did have breast implants. Since that had nothing to do with the trial, I can only think it was contrived to embarrass me. But it did not. I am truly glad that I had my breasts redone and I believe that any woman who's not happy with her body should take whatever steps she can to feel better about herself.

It must have dismayed Cochran when Judge Ito ruled that Christian Reichardt could not testify about my past drug use. The defense team was set to discredit me and every word that I had written in *Private Diary*. But, on the grounds that there was absolutely no evidence to support the Dream Team's contention that Nicole's death was drug related, Judge Ito upheld the prosecution's motion to suppress any information on my drug use that might come from Christian. If he had been permitted to testify on that subject, it would have been one long lie. Christian had never talked to or even seen anyone who sold me drugs. He had seen me doing drugs a total of three times, two of which were with him.

Christian was so upset by Judge Ito's ruling that, when he left the courtroom, he stood in the parking lot giving interviews to the press, speculating about how I got drugs. He said since I didn't have money to pay for them, he had to conclude that Nicole's murder must have had something to do with a drug hit and he was going to get to the bottom of it.

One of his friends was murdered, another was being tried for committing two murders, and he suddenly believed that this was connected with a drug hit and he wanted to get to the bottom of it? Was he crazy or what?

Another statement of Johnnie Cochran's was that I did not have a job. Much to my regret, I worked for Christian in his chiropractic office because he insisted on it. Although Dr. Reichardt never got around to paying me because he claimed that he never had enough money, I was, theoretically, earning a salary. Fortunately, I did not need it.

The defense had put me on their witness list, and when they decided to have me served with a subpoena, they did it in the cruelest way possible. They knew my address, and as I was at home much of the time, they could have found me there without any problem. Instead, they chose to serve me when I was, as I am many Sundays, at a West Los Angeles park watching Francesca play softball.

In what was clearly an attempt to embarrass me in front of my daughter, her friends, and their parents, a process server handed me a paper directing me to appear before Superior Court Judge Lance A. Ito on July 3. The defense knew very well that there would be no court session the day before Independence Day—that is my birthday, and I believe it was O.J.'s way of trying to spoil it for me. As long as the trial continued, I knew that I was fair game for anything they could manufacture about me that might conceivably help O.J.

Cochran made a great point of stressing that O.J. was not physically capable of having committed the murders because of his arthritis. That's amazing. O.J. was able to play golf, and one week earlier, as O.J. mentioned in his statement to Detectives Vannatter and Lang about the last time he had been at Nicole's house, he had been chasing Kato the dog. I was on that chase, too, and I couldn't keep up with O.J. In fact, I had told him how impressed I was that he could run so fast.

Johnnie Cochran and O.J. have a great deal in common. They both led dual lives. Cochran comes off as a model lawyer and civic leader, but it is a matter of public record that he has been living a lie. While he was legally married to one woman, he proposed to another, had a child (Johnnie Cochran III!) with her, supported her and their child, and had frequent sexual encounters with her over a period of eighteen years. I'm sure it did not gladden Cochran's heart when his mistress went on "Geraldo" and confided, "Johnnie said, 'Just give me one black person on the jury and I'll get a hung jury.'"

O.J. also lived a lie. His public image was that of one of the most charming and charismatic men to ever walk the face of this earth, and he played that role very well. But he could never be faithful to his wife, and behind closed doors he could be a raging monster.

So Johnnie Cochran, the respected lawyer, had no problem standing behind O.J. Simpson, the innocent hero. Not everything he did for O.J. was a first for him. Attacking the Los Angeles Police Department, for example, had been one of the tactics he had used for several of his clients over the years. Perhaps it is one of the secrets of his success.

There was a lot of discussion about the racial aspects of this case. But that should not have been an issue. The question before the jury was whether or not O.J. Simpson was guilty of the murder of Nicole Brown Simpson and Ron Goldman. The color of his skin—or theirs—should not have entered into it. Unfortunately it did.

It was evident that to some extent public perception of O.J.'s guilt or innocence was divided along racial lines. A large percentage of African Americans seemed to believe he was innocent. Many others, however, were convinced of his guilt.

At Agape Church one Sunday, I told the Reverend Dr. Michael Beckwith, an incredible man, how much peace he brought to my life through his sermons and teachings. Through his sermons, I was able to separate myself from the trial. His energy was serene and pure. He told me to stay on the path and keep spreading light. I promised him I would. As I was leaving, an African-American member of the church approached me and said he wanted to give me a message. "Do not take personally any criticism from the black community. Although many blacks realize that O.J. is guilty, to see a black man use the system to his advantage and buy his way to freedom as the white man has done for centuries gives some of us a sense of satisfaction."

I heard the message loud and clear, and I thanked him for his honesty. The thinking he described is what Johnnie Cochran counted on, but it had no place within this trial. The trial was to determine whether or not O.J. Simpson had murdered two people, regardless of the color of his skin.

To be fair, we have to look at the history of prejudice in too many police departments throughout the United States. It is no secret—in fact, it is a national disgrace—that minorities have been subjected to unfounded and inexcusable police brutality throughout the decades. There is a countless number of documented incidents of such treatment and undoubtedly there are many, many more that are undocumented. And that continues to this day. We can just think back to the Rodney King case in Los Angeles to know how ruthless the police can be. And O.J.'s defense team took every opportunity to remind the jury that O.J. Simpson may have been subjected to the same prejudiced police force.

Practically every time we pick up a newspaper, we read an account of some form of racial prejudice committed against a minority, most often a black person. African Americans know that when a police officer sees a black man with a white woman, subconscious or outright prejudice may become a factor. We also know that too many of our police are capable of acting on their instincts, not their intelligence. So it was not outrageous that awareness of this deplorable fact would enter into judgments about O.J.'s guilt.

Johnnie Cochran took these factors into account when he prepared his defense. Part of his reason may have been based on what he knew of the record of the L.A. Police Department. But undoubtedly his major motivation was to sway the African Americans on the jury.

We know that every lawyer walks into court wanting to win his or her case. Yet we shouldn't expect a defense lawyer to disregard all ethical and human considerations to absolve a client of a crime. It was obvious that Cochran wanted to win at any price. And he did!

Even though Cochran's techniques and objectives were so transparent that no thinking person could doubt them, they were seldom if ever discussed by the legal analysts or the media. I think it's because although Cochran didn't hesitate to suggest that the whole O.J. trial was a racial conspiracy, anyone who dared to criticize Cochran risked being designated a racist.

For me, one of the most painful aspects of the trial and the public reaction to it was the extent to which Cochran was able to plant the suggestion that Nicole deserved to be killed. In the first place, there is nothing anyone, much less Nicole, could do that would justify paying the death penalty at the hands of her husband. The fact that I have had to defend Nicole against such insinuations is frightening. Not only have hostile audiences implied as much, but even seemingly reasonable members of the media have asked questions that raised that issue.

As the end of the trial neared, Cochran seemed to become even more desperate and dangerous. As he asked the population of Los Angeles to try to remain calm and control their anger at the possibility of a guilty verdict, it seemed that he was, both subtly and overtly, provoking unrest. It's incredible that he could have lost sight of the great harm that has been done to both blacks and whites alike by past demonstrations in Los Angeles. Our country has spent decades trying to undo past inequities and bring people of all races together in unity. It's amazing that any "responsible" citizen would, at every opportunity, be so divisive and destructive.

At times Cochran seemed to enthrall the jury. He dazzled them with speeches planned to blind them to the truth and to soften their hearts and minds toward his client. Two of the dismissed jurors said that they and their fellow jurors were "mesmerized" by Cochran. It is frightening to think that even one juror would be susceptible to his power of suggestion and fail to see through his deceit.

Even more horrifying is the statement going around that O.J. Simpson and Johnnie Cochran have made wife beating socially acceptable and that many batterers may now decide that they can get away with killing their wives.

ROBERT KARDASHIAN

Although Robert Kardashian was never heard from in court, he was a key member of the defense team. He would be more than willing to defend O.J. under any circumstances. He had retired as a successful music industry executive and although he was a lawyer, he had not practiced law for twenty years. He reactivated his law practice after the murder, and it has been suggested that he did it so that he could conceal evidence and wouldn't be forced to testify. It is my guess that when O.J. stayed at Robert's house in Encino instead of going home when he returned from Chicago, they were busy developing their elaborate schemes.

A few days after Nicole's death, Robert started floating rumors that some Colombians were after me. He called his ex-wife Kris Jenner and told her and then she called Christian. Of course, Robert told the defense at the first opportunity. They really picked up on that, but nobody who had ever known Nicole or me believed it—and I doubt that the defense did, either.

Starting that rumor was just Robert Kardashian's way of muddying the waters, and if that was not enough, Robert embellished it further by claiming that Nicole and I had borrowed money from the Colombian cartel to finance the coffee bar we had talked about opening. He explained to Kris and our other friends that Nicole was murdered because we didn't have the money to pay the cartel back.

Robert also tried to help the defense when he became involved in O.J.'s shell game with his baggage. When O.J. returned from Chicago, a TV crew filmed Robert picking up O.J.'s Louis Vuitton valet bag. I guess no one will ever know what actually happened to it. All that we know is that when it was turned over to the court, it was empty. And there is a question as to whether that was even the actual bag that O.J. had taken. Everybody in our group had one or more bags like that—it would have been easy to turn in a substitute.

When Robert was originally asked what happened to the Vuitton bag that he had been seen on TV taking from O.J. after he returned from Chicago, Robert said he had no idea. How can a man pick up a Louis Vuitton garment bag and take it to his home and then not know where it is? The original bag could have held the clothing O.J. had worn or other important clues or trace evidence.

There was also the black bag that O.J. took with him and refused to let the limousine driver load—O.J. wanted to put it in the car himself. Whenever O.J. went anywhere in a limousine, the driver always handled all the baggage. Why was that little black bag so important to O.J. that he picked it up himself?

The limousine driver in Los Angeles said the bag looked full when O.J. left Brentwood, but when O.J. arrived in Chicago, according to the limousine driver who met him there, when the driver picked that bag up, it was so light that it seemed as if there was little or nothing in it. Obviously, O.J.

had gotten rid of the contents—probably his blood-spattered clothing—in one of the airports. Why did it appear full when the first limousine driver saw it and empty when the limousine driver in Chicago handled it?

What about the golf bag that didn't come back from Chicago until one day later, and why did O.J. and Robert Kardashian go all the way to the airport to pick it up together? O.J. had just lost his ex-wife and now all of a sudden he was running to the airport concerned about his golf bag.

When the prosecution showed that particular bag to the limo driver during direct examination, the driver said that it was not the same golf bag at all! Again this did not surprise me because if you ever went into O.J.'s garage you would have found many golf bags. Let's not forget that appearing at golf tournaments was part of his job as a spokesman for Hertz Corporation.

I'd like to know why the golf bag that was turned in to the prosecution was not the one that O.J. had taken to Chicago. Was it because he had hidden the knife in the golf bag among the metal clubs so the metal detectors would not have picked it up? Perhaps there was some evidence of blood in both the golf bag and the Louis Vuitton bag. If, as A.C. is supposed to have told his girlfriend, the knife was hidden in the golf bag, that was an inspired maneuver. There is so much metal in a golf bag that it would never have been detected by airport security.

So these things are in question: The golf bag that O.J. had taken to Chicago was not the golf bag that was turned over to the D.A., and the original golf bag has never been accounted for; the small black bag that O.J. would not let anyone touch has never turned up; and the Louis Vuitton bag that Robert Kardashian so casually strolled away with was turned in empty, and may not even have been the right bag.

Unfortunately the tension between Robert and me has created a sad situation for Francesca and Robert and Kris's daughter, Khloe Kardashian, who were best friends. Before the horrors of the murders and the trial, Khloe and Francesca spent all their time together, but because I had felt he had been so destructive, I did not want her to go to the Kardashians' house. If it hadn't been so distressing, it would have been funny. At the same time that Robert Kardashian was telling the public that I was the real target of the murderer and that the Cali cartel was still after me, Robert's children would sometimes come to play with Francesca and stay overnight at my house. If he had even suspected that there was any basis for that rumor, I am sure he would not have allowed his children to be in such a dangerous situation. I am also sure that when the defense team learned that Robert Kardashian's daughter was often at my house, they realized they had to stop using that ploy. Cheri Lewis of the prosecution team put it this way: "There is no basis for those allegations. If there are drug dealers out there ready to kill Faye Resnick, why is she still alive? And why does Robert Kardashian think it's safe for Khloe and Robert Kardashian, Jr., to sleep at her house?"

Neither Kris Jenner nor I wanted our children mentioned in the trial, but I couldn't help being glad that the truth had been put in the record. I see Robert now and then, but I speak to him only when necessary, for example, when I was arranging to take Khloe and Francesca to the Ice Capades, or to say when I would pick Khloe up or drop her off. Every Sunday I would go to Francesca's softball game. Khloe was also on the team. Robert would sometimes ask if I would take Khloe home because he had to go to court. (I had never been aware that the courts were open on Sunday.) Anyway, Khloe has always been like my second child, so of course I was glad to take her home.

The most memorable time our paths crossed was one day when I was leaving the D.A.'s office. Detective Philip Vannatter and I were in the elevator at the courthouse. It stopped at the fourth floor and Robert Kardashian started to get on. He saw me and reached out to give me a hug. From just outside the elevator, Johnnie Cochran saw Robert leaning toward me. He grabbed Robert's coat and literally pulled him out of the elevator. There were a lot of people around and Cochran didn't want anyone to see Robert Kardashian hugging Faye Resnick. But they did see Cochran pulling on Robert's coattails. It must have been quite a sight for the spectators—one short man tugging at another short man to rescue him from a woman even shorter than either of them.

F. LEE BAILEY

Another sterling member of the defense team was F. Lee Bailey. Although nobody would have suspected it from the way he and Robert Shapiro seemed to feud at times, Bailey was the godfather of one of Robert Shapiro's children. The whole time he was in the courtroom, Bailey looked as if he were dying for a vodka tonic. It appeared that he was an alcoholic who desperately needed a drink, and everyone felt very sorry for him. As for his claims about the L.A. Police Department's well-planned conspiracy to frame O.J., on the one hand, it would be surprising to learn that the L.A.P.D. could always work so quickly and be so skillful. On the other hand, Bailey was—to the amazement of many, but not to a large segment of the African-American population—right on target about Mark Fuhrman. That unprincipled, lying bigot had a lot of people fooled. One of the best things that came out of the O.J. Simpson trial is the vastly increased public awareness of the bigotry and injustice that continues to exist in our police departments and, therefore, in our judicial system.

Still, I can't help remembering that O.J. was a hero to members of the L.A.P.D. I was with O.J. the night when he was so crazed that the manager of the restaurant called the police. When the police saw who he was, they bent over backward to be nice to him. And Nicole repeatedly said that it didn't do any good to call the police when O.J. was beating her because they were always so impressed to meet him that they couldn't do enough for him. They let him get away with everything. Wherever he went, policemen asked for his autograph and told him how much they admired him. These were the people Johnnie Cochran and his cohorts suspected of setting up—in a matter of minutes—an elaborate conspiracy against O.J.

ROBERT SHAPIRO

At a certain point the defense team seemed to add concern for their own reputations to their concern for O.J. I have to admit that when Robert

Shapiro wore a blue ribbon to denote his support of the L.A.P.D. and said that he had never agreed with introducing the racial element into the case, I saw a glimmer of integrity in him and felt he was embarrassed to be a part of those tactics. From what I hear, he's sorry that he ever became involved with the trial, but I guess, for his own image and career, he needed to follow through. While I do have a bit of compassion for Shapiro, it is only a bit. After all, it was Robert Shapiro who, with the help of Robert Kardashian and O.J. Simpson, furthered the rumor that Nicole's murder was a drug hit directed at me. I will always hold him responsible for that.

My friend Kathy Hilton—a woman I respect and like very much—and her husband, Rick, are good friends with Robert Shapiro. I was amazed when she said, "Robert Shapiro really admires you very much. When this trial is all over, is it possible that you would join us for dinner with him and his wife?"

She and I were having dinner at Mr. Chow's in Beverly Hills and we knew half the people there. The last thing I wanted was to have anyone see me crying. Tears came streaming down my face and I said, "Kathy, how could you even ask me that question? That man was willing to put my life and my child's life in jeopardy by floating that incredibly destructive false rumor about me. He never stopped to think that it was my future he was playing with. The thought of sitting across the table from him is upsetting and it hurts me that you would even ask me to do such a thing."

Kathy was truly sorry, and when she later called to apologize again, she said, "I guess I didn't really understand that this is real. So many people look at it as a form of entertainment now."

I said, "Well, it is very real to me. This is not a joke or a form of entertainment. It is a grim reality. Nicole was my dearest, closest friend. All of us who cared about her have been robbed of her presence. Most of all, her children have been robbed of their mother, who loved them so much. I will never dine with anyone who has had anything to do with trying to set her murderer free."

One night I had just joined my friends at Drai's when Victor Drai approached me. That was nothing unusual about that—he was always very cordial to me—but this time he had a different look on his face. Victor said that Robert Shapiro was dining in the back and would like to meet me. He asked me if he could bring Shapiro to my table. I quickly replied, "Absolutely not, Victor! I have no interest in meeting Robert Shapiro." Victor appeared baffled by my abrupt response, but said he understood.

Later that evening, as our group was in the midst of an interesting conversation, enjoying cappuccinos and listening to a progressive jazz group, I was beginning to think that maybe I could again enjoy relaxing with friends. Then I glanced up to see Robert Shapiro walking toward my table. I looked away, hoping to avoid the situation, but he insisted on being introduced. All I could think of at that moment was how would Nicole feel, and what would she do? As Shapiro put out his hand, I said, "I'm sorry, I cannot shake hands with you." And I turned away.

KATO KAELIN

Of all the people who have supported O.J., Kato Kaelin stands as one of the biggest liars. It is well known that what he said on the witness stand was the complete opposite of what he said on the tapes he made for a book he was planning to co-author. He testified that on the night of the murder O.J. acted perfectly normal. But on the transcripts of the tapes, he told the truth: that Nicole had told him many times that she was afraid that O.J. would kill her, and, as he told many people around him, O.J. was acting very strange that night.

On the witness stand, Kato was shaking and looked as if he were on drugs. He was very fast to say that he had never done cocaine or any other drug, but he certainly had all the symptoms. The prosecution knew that Kato had talked about how upset O.J. had been the night of the murders, so they considered his testimony extremely significant.

But when he was on the witness stand it became clear that he had done an about-face. Maybe he decided he didn't want to harm O.J.'s case. Or maybe he thought about what might happen to him if O.J. went free and wanted to even the score.

Kato was telling the truth when he said that he was not Nicole's lover. Contrary to what the tabloids were trumpeting, Nicole never had the slightest romantic or sexual interest in Kato. He had always been known as a professional house guest—he did not seem to have a home of his own—and he had been staying at her house. He was wonderful with the children and that was one of the reasons why she continued to let him stay there. He was unable to pay rent, but he was a great babysitter.

When Kato was testifying that O.J. had asked him to move to O.J.'s house, he denied that O.J. had been upset at him for living with Nicole. He said that O.J. just didn't feel it was right for a man to be living with a woman under any circumstances. Kato was not living with Nicole: He was living in her guest house. When the prosecution asked him if Nicole felt betrayed by his moving out, he said, "No, she did not."

I was there when Nicole told Kato that he was betraying her, that they had made an arrangement and she was counting on him. He was starting to make a little money and they had agreed that he would either pay rent or continue babysitting for the children. Either way, she benefited by having him live there. She liked the fact that there was a man around. She felt that the reason O.J. hadn't beat her again after the 1993 incident, when they taped O.J. screaming at Nicole while she was on the phone to the police, was that Kato was nearby. So she found security in having him at the house.

When Kato coolly denied that Nicole had minded when he left, I sat there in disbelief. I had heard Nicole tell him, "I never want to talk to you again. You have been taken in by O.J. He has made you a better offer, but you were supposedly my friend. We had a deal, and once again my life is being manipulated by O.J. I don't want that in my life and I don't want you anywhere around me again." Nicole also told that to CiCi Shahian. Kato was just outright lying.

After he testified, Kato went outside to the reporters and his statement was, "People forget that I lost a very dear friend." He did not lose his very dear friend on June 12. He lost Nicole as a friend the day he moved out of her house, and he knew that. From the day Kato moved in with O.J., Nicole wanted nothing to do with him. The only time she would even speak to him was when he answered the phone at O.J.'s or when they were in the presence of the children.

Nicole always kept her word. When she decided to cut anyone out of her life, she would do just that. She was a very loyal friend and she expected her friends to be the same way with her. If she had reason to believe that someone was disloyal, she would just shut down immediately.

There is another rumor that never went very far. The story was that when O.J. returned from the murder scene, he tried to sneak in the house over the back fence. He realized he had dropped a glove and went to look for it. As this was going on Kato heard what he described as three thumps coming from the wall near the back gate. He went to check out the noise and saw O.J. standing there. O.J. knew that Kato would not be a problem—he would say whatever O.J. told him to say. But O.J. was concerned about the limo driver seeing him, which is why he concocted the story about his nighttime golf practice.

It was Kato's report about hearing the thumps that led to the discovery of the bloody glove. Kato later told friends that he had seen O.J. out there that night, but he did not mention it in his testimony. It must have been a great disappointment to the defense when Kato slipped and told the truth on the tapes he made for the book he was planning to write. Although Kato testified that O.J. had been in a good mood the night of the murders, on the tape Kato said that O.J. had been very upset. When confronted, Kato said that the person who taped his interviews had put words in his mouth. On a tape?

Kato managed to slip another lie into his testimony. When prosecutor Marcia Clark asked if he was planning to write a book, Kato said he had been approached, but had decided not to do it. At some point he had had a dispute with the writer he made the tapes with and then tried to say he had nothing to do with the book. But the author used those tapes, the book came out, and there was some talk about whether or not Kato was guilty of perjury.

We'll never know all the lies that Kato managed to tell, but we know for sure that he lied.

A.C. COWLINGS

A.C. Cowlings, O.J.'s boyhood friend and close buddy, is another member of the liars club. Although he has always lied and covered up for O.J., you have to give him credit for being a loyal friend. There can be little doubt that, regardless of

the circumstances, A.C. would do anything—
anything—he could to help O.J.

A.C.'s life and identity always revolved around
O.J. O.J. has always supported him, so it is
understandable that he would go out of his way to
avoid biting the hand that has fed him year in and
year out. They were together often and they
enjoyed exchanging outfits and devising other
ways to dodge the press. A.C. loved the limelight
that came with being around O.J. O.J. used A.C.
and A.C. used O.J. and that was their deal.

After he and O.J. finished leading the caravan
in the Bronco, A.C. stayed pretty much in the
background with the exception of the Ask A.C.
900 phone line that people could call to talk
about O.J. for $2.99 a minute. By the time they
got to their questions, they had spent $5 or $6 to
hear about how O.J. was totally innocent.
According to *U.S. News and World Report*, A.C.
made $300,000 in the first thirty days. The last I
heard, A.C. was selling autographs at a meeting
of sports card collectors.

A.C. must have said the wrong thing to the
wrong person. The word went out that A.C. had
said to his girlfriend that "the knife is swimming
with the fish" and that he was certain that O.J.
was the murderer, but it never came out in the

trial. And we can be sure A.C. would deny that with his hand on a stack of Bibles. As long as they both shall live, O.J. will know that he has at least one friend who will always do anything and everything he could ever ask.

MARCUS ALLEN

Marcus Allen was often described as a younger, handsomer O.J. Simpson. He is very charming and women find him extremely attractive. He was O.J.'s protégé. I particularly remember the time Marcus had a fight with Al Davis, owner of the former Los Angeles Raiders, and O.J. was right there to protect him. There was a rumor that the reason for that fight was that Marcus was having a fling with someone Davis didn't approve of. Marcus doesn't mean any harm, but women are vulnerable to him and he is vulnerable to women.

Marcus did not show up for Nicole's funeral, but that was probably because he was too upset to be there. I believe that Marcus loved Nicole in many ways and that his loyalties were with her. Time and again, I heard him say, "For God's sake, Nicole, why do you put up with O.J.'s abuse? That just isn't right!" And that was in the days when O.J. had stopped beating her for a while and was just abusing her verbally. So, perhaps Marcus was, in his own way, protecting Nicole by staying away. I'm sure he also was protecting himself and his career.

Marcus flat out told the prosecution that he had never had a romantic relationship with Nicole. His attorney and agent, Ed Hookstratten, who is now also Robert Shapiro's agent, repeatedly said that Marcus had never been involved with Nicole in any way. And he threatened to sue me for saying otherwise in *Private Diary*. Hookstratten must have found out that my version was 100 percent true, because that suit never materialized. But he never changed his story.

However, that version did not fit in with the defense team's strategy. They went to great lengths to explain that even though O.J. knew all about that affair, he had still permitted Marcus to have his wedding at the Rockingham house. Their point seemed to be that O.J. was such an easygoing, kind, and tolerant person that he didn't mind that Nicole and Marcus had been lovers after he and Nicole were divorced.

I heard what O.J. said as the wedding was being arranged, and it was very clear that he was being so magnanimous only because Marcus had promised that after he was married he would never go near Nicole again. Since O.J. was monitoring his ex-wife very carefully, he may have discovered that Marcus and Nicole were still getting together after his marriage. That was during the time that Nicole was telling O.J. that she and O.J. were definitely finished, that she wanted nothing more to do with him and he should stay away from her.

It was public knowledge, at least in our group, that Marcus was beyond incredible in bed. O.J. knew that, too, and that may be what pushed him over the edge. He was humiliated and very, very angry.

Angry enough to commit murder.

The defense tried to subpoena Marcus, but he lived in Kansas City and managed to avoid testifying. Marcus has always been very conscious of protecting his image and he may also have been protecting his marriage. Maybe that's why he was so careful to stay away. He was not making any appearances or giving any interviews, and it was obvious that he just wanted to keep out of it.

There is also another possibility: Marcus may have been afraid that under cross-examination, he might get cornered into admitting that he believed that O.J. had murdered Nicole. And Marcus knew what could happen to people who humiliate and anger O.J.

PART IV

Justice?

The earnest and constant will to render every man his due. The precepts of the law are these: to live honorably, to injure no other man, to render to every man his due.

—Justinian I

Chapter 13

THE PROSECUTION

LOS ANGELES, CALIFORNIA
JANUARY–OCTOBER 1995

I kept saying to the prosecution, "Isn't it possible for me to go to court? We really need to let the jury know that Nicole was a warm and wonderful human being who is no longer among us." That's what CiCi, Robin, and I wanted to do. As the trial progressed, I also thought it was important for them to know that Nicole's friend Faye Resnick was a respectable, responsible woman, not a degenerate drug addict. But that, too, was out of the question.

I knew that if I had been murdered, Nicole would have done everything in her power to be there for me. But I couldn't be there in court for her because at first I was on the witness list for the prosecution and then I was on the witness list for the defense, and this prevented me from sitting in on the trial. As Nicole's closest friends were on the witness list of either the prosecution or the defense, it was left up to the Browns to remind the jury of Nicole by attending the trial.

At the beginning Nicole's family was at the trial fairly often, but as time went on they attended less and less frequently. It was a great distance from their home and sitting in that courtroom must have been very painful for them. But I still felt that a reminder that Nicole was a real person should be before the jury at all times. Fortunately Ron Goldman's sister was able to be in that courtroom practically every single day and his parents were there very often, so there was some ongoing reminder of the humanity of the victims.

Ron's father, a kind and brilliant man, said, "We sit here to remind the jury that this case is not only about O.J. Simpson, but about a lovely woman and a fine young man who were brutally murdered."

If Nicole had been able to see the mockery of justice that went on in that courtroom and the way O.J. allowed the defense to paint her as a party girl, she would not have been the least surprised. It was just what she had anticipated. She had told both

CiCi Shahian and me that O.J. would try to ruin the lives of anyone who dared to cross him.

One thing I can say for O.J. Simpson is that he does keep his word. He said he would murder Nicole and he did. He said he'd get away with it, and he did by directing his defense team to dig up any type of scandal and put up any kind of smoke screen that might divert attention from his heinous act. O.J. always thought that making others look bad made him look good. Whenever things were not going O.J.'s way, he would immediately bring up somebody else's scandal. That was his pattern even before he murdered Nicole.

Nicole really called it. She was the smartest of us all. She knew exactly what was going to happen and must have thought she was protecting herself by documenting the abuse, but she neglected to do the one thing that could have saved her. She did not get away from O.J. before it was too late.

* * *

Throughout the trial, I had the utmost respect for the prosecution team that was, in my mind, defending Nicole and Ron. Both Marcia Clark and Chris Darden struck me as very forthright, honest, intelligent, and capable professionals. I also felt that they did not expect the defense to be so totally unprincipled, and that made me very uneasy.

During one of our early meetings (and I still don't know how I had the nerve to do it), I urged Marcia Clark to change the venue of the trial from Los Angeles to Santa Monica, which would have been logical and, I believe, infinitely more fair. Marcia assured me that because O.J. was 110 percent guilty, they would do equally well in L.A.—that they would have a clear-cut guilty verdict regardless of where O.J. was tried. I sometimes wonder if Marcia remembers that conversation and regrets not having taken more seriously my assurances that O.J. would have his defense team go beyond any limits she could ever imagine. In fact, I believe that one of the reasons the defense was able to get away with what they did was that the prosecution simply did not believe that O.J.'s lawyers would use such devious and questionable tactics. They just did not think in those terms.

Marcia had not lost a case in five years, and both she and Chris Darden were prepared to work around the clock if necessary. Although there were many references to the resources of the prosecution team, that was fiction. They did not have anything even remotely resembling the support available to the defense. The defense team had their staffs at their disposal, plus the time and effort of the dozens of interns and students Alan Dershowitz had assigned to support various aspects of the defense team's strategies.

Aside from the tactics and sheer numbers of their opposition, both Clark and Darden were subjected to personal attacks designed to divert their efforts from their primary focus. Whereas a male lawyer with her strength and conviction would have been described as a strong and dedicated prosecutor, Clark was described variously as "cold," "hard," and "a bitch." To complicate her life further, her ex-husband chose that time to decide that he should have custody of their children. Every working mother knows that there are times when her workload will divert too much time from her children, and manages to find ways to fulfill her responsibilities in spite of that burden. Clark was no exception to that problem, but the opportunity to harass and embarrass her must have been irresistible to her ex-husband.

Chris Darden, a kind and somewhat emotional man, has a reputation as an excellent lawyer, but these are facts that seem to have little to do with the issues that confronted him. I gather that he and Johnnie Cochran had been friends, that

Darden had looked up to him as a role model of sorts. But it was rumored that one of Cochran's media buddies arranged for a tabloid story on Darden and his family, and that their friendship may have evaporated. I understand that in an interview Darden indicated that he was so disillusioned by what he saw in the Simpson trial that he was questioning whether he wanted to continue in his chosen field.

Every time the defense would present a new theory or strategy, the prosecution seemed overwhelmed, obviously not accustomed to dealing with people who were willing to stop at nothing to defend their client's and their own reputations. Very early on in the trial, it became clear that the defense team considered the question of their client's guilt or innocence less important than the furthering of their careers and the protection of their ostensible respectability.

It is understandable that the prosecution may have been intimidated by this group of high-powered, highly devious so-called officers of the court. I don't believe that they had ever been confronted with a team as high profile as F. Lee Bailey, Barry Scheck, Johnnie Cochran, Alan Dershowitz, and Robert Shapiro. These men have been in the game for many years and among them they could come up with more defense strategies than there are days in the year.

The prosecution did not function that way. They used a very honest and direct approach. They wanted to show the evidence and they were confident that, based upon that evidence, it would be clear to any jury that O.J. Simpson was guilty.

For some reason the prosecution did not make good use of all the ammunition that was available to them. One reason may be that every time they introduced another point, it opened up a whole new avenue of attack for the defense. The defense seemed able to turn anything the prosecution did into a sideshow, and it seems that the prosecution became intimidated.

A good example of a missed opportunity was the keys that disappeared from Nicole's house. One week before Nicole was murdered I had become convinced that O.J. was getting so out of hand that he might actually follow through on his threat to kill Nicole, so I left her house to stay with my friend Kathy. I begged Nicole to come with me, but she insisted that she and the children would be fine.

Wanting to give me a set of keys to her house, she went to get the ones she always used to get in through her back gate. Nicole came dashing back into the room and said, "Oh my God, the keys are not there! I'll bet anything that O.J. took them when he was here last week." She went through the house and couldn't find them, and then she saw that the duplicate remote to her garage also was missing and realized that O.J. had taken that, too. She told five different friends that she felt very nervous because O.J. had her keys. And all of us, including Elvie, the housekeeper, searched for those keys and the remote for a week without success.

The prosecution knew this, but they never brought it up. They knew that O.J. was able to get into Nicole's back gate, go around front, and slice her neck. And how did he do that? He didn't jump the fence—he opened the gate with the keys that he stole from Nicole's house. CiCi Shahian, Kris Jenner, Elvie, and I could have testified that those keys were missing and that Nicole was upset because she knew that O.J. had them. That should have been explained to the jury.

They did bring up the IRS letter, which was given to Nicole the Sunday before her death. They had CiCi Shahian on the witness stand to verify that the letter threatening that O.J. would report Nicole to the IRS was sent to Nicole from O.J.'s attorney. But they did not go into the psychological ramifications of it. They simply asked CiCi to confirm that what they were showing her was the letter that O.J. had sent to Nicole stating that since she no longer wanted to be in his life, he was taking steps that would result in her losing the house in which she and her children were living.

When O.J. called me and announced that he was going to send that letter, I said, "How dare you even think about doing something like that to the mother of your children?" The letter stated that O.J. was going to contact the IRS and inform them that Nicole was no longer living with him on Rockingham. That meant that she would have had to pay a capital gains tax of $90,000, which was exactly the amount Nicole had in the bank when she died. And she would have had to sell her home after just moving the children in and find a new place for them to live—which was what she had planned to do eventually, but those things take some time and planning.

To set the record straight: Nicole was not trying to cheat the IRS. She was under financial pressure. She had bought the Bundy condominium and was planning to rent it, intending to live with O.J. at the Rockingham house. But after that became impossible, she moved herself and the children into the condominium until she could find something she could afford. O.J. knew that, but he was showing how pissed off he was becoming with her as he realized that their relationship was really over.

There were many psychological implications in the whole scenario that would have added to the picture of what was going on in O.J.'s mind. Nicole was upset that O.J. would be so spiteful to her, but was furious that he would do something that could disrupt her children's lives by uprooting them again.

After CiCi had testified, the prosecution should have asked her about Nicole's fears toward the end of her life, or about the jewelry Nicole had given back to O.J., or even about the fact that Nicole had given O.J. the videotape of their wedding, something she had always treasured, saying that she no longer wanted to remember it. There was so much more that CiCi should have been asked. She really knew what had been going on, and she is completely reliable and would have been able to stand up under any cross-examination.

I don't recall that the prosecution brought up the fact that Nicole had just added a codicil to her will, but it could have been significant that a thirty-five-year-old woman was concerned with her will. I didn't make a will until after Nicole died. I did then because I was so afraid that O.J. would have me killed and I wanted whatever I had to go to my daughter.

The prosecution did not know that Nicole had documented O.J.'s abuse until the Brown family found her diary, and even then they were able to have only a small part of the information put in the record. It would seem that they should have had somebody besides Denise Brown, who might have been considered biased because she was Nicole's sister, testify about the abuse. Why didn't they call Linda Schulman to the witness stand? She had been close to Nicole and O.J. until their divorce; she knew all about the beatings.

There was just too much relevant information that the prosecution did not use. They spent eight days questioning a coroner who was not even the person who actually viewed the body. It seems they could have spent some time showing exactly what went on in the month before the murders.

And then there was Juditha Brown. Although O.J. often confided in me, it was well known that Juditha was O.J.'s closest confidante. For the entire time that he and Nicole were married, O.J. used Juditha as his sounding board, but all the prosecution had Juditha do was give a brief statement concerning her last phone call with

Nicole in which Juditha mentioned her missing eyeglasses. She had so much more to offer the prosecution in the way of revealing information.

It is my understanding that most of this evidence would have been admissible in court, and I believe that the prosecution should have used it. Perhaps there were reasons why they did not. In Juditha's case, they may have felt there were skeletons in her closet—There was once a rumor that she and O.J. had been closer than inlaws—and maybe Juditha was reluctant to testify. But the truth is the truth—you state it and if you have to face a tough cross-examination, you deal with it.

They were afraid to have me testify because of my drug history. But that was in the record, anyway, and Judge Ito had made it clear that he did not consider it important. The fact remains that I knew what was going on in O.J.'s head. I knew what he had been thinking, and he had told me what he was planning to do. I knew what Nicole was feeling in the last month and so did Juditha, Denise, and CiCi. These are the people who knew exactly what had been building up and were trying to save Nicole's life.

CiCi, Robin, and I kept saying, "It's okay because they will go back to the domestic violence issue when they get through with the other evidence."

But, instead, the prosecution rested their case. We wanted to scream, "Why are you stopping now?" There was so much that the jury never heard about. The jury needed to hear what really happened. They needed to know what Nicole was going through. They needed to hear that this woman truly feared for her life, but wouldn't flee because of her children. She was trying to build a stable life for them, so she couldn't avoid contact with their father. The jury needed to hear that, and CiCi, Juditha, and I had all that information at our fingertips.

The fact that the prosecution never touched on O.J.'s drug use was another major mistake. They could have shown that this man, O.J. Simpson, was not the perfect person his image conveyed but an abuser of both his wife and drugs. They had evidence of that at their fingertips, but although they permitted my drug use to be raised time and again, they never introduced the subject in connection with O.J.

While I have great respect for the concept of American justice, I am deeply disturbed—in fact, heartsick—over the way the system seems to work. I understand that it is vital to protect the rights of a defendant, but more often than not we seem to totally discount the rights of the victim. It is becoming increasingly clear that the scales of justice weigh differently for the rich and the poor, and for the famous and the obscure. Time and again, we see people who are clearly guilty of crimes being found not guilty in spite of overwhelming evidence. It seems that those who can afford a high-powered lawyer—or several of them—are untouchable. Justice should not be for sale!

If it had been anyone except O.J., it would have been an open-and-shut case, but the combination of what some consider O.J.'s charm and a defense team that seemed determined to stop at nothing added up to an unbeatable opponent. I cannot help feeling bitter about their attacks on me. I acknowledge that I used drugs (please note "used"—that is definitely in the past tense). But I have never for a moment been the immoral, indecent person they portrayed with their lies, nor was there any way I was remotely responsible for Nicole's death.

There is little question that Judge Ito's handling of the O.J. Simpson case will be written into the annals of judicial history. I look forward to hearing some of the conclusions that will be reached. Although I will leave the analysis of his conduct of the case to academics in the legal profession, I can't help raising a point or two.

There was one inconsistency that bothered me considerably. Early in the trial some of Nicole's friends and others started wearing tiny gold angel pins to express their feelings for her. I gather that the Brown family gave one to prosecutor Marcia Clark and she appeared in court with it on her lapel. Judge Ito immediately instructed her to remove it, saying there were to be no signals of bias in his court. Months later the defense team appeared in court wearing identical African-print ties as a show of solidarity. Judge Ito made no comment. I can't imagine that he was able to spy a tiny angel pin and not observe those symbolic ties. If he didn't understand the symbolism, he might have inquired about it. Or maybe Judge Ito had given up on trying to keep signals of bias out of his court.

It was obvious that Judge Ito was a well-intentioned man and under normal circumstances may be an excellent judge. But the O.J. Simpson trial was not normal by any measure known to the many authorities I met as the trial progressed. And I will always wonder how much the cameras in the courtroom changed the procedure. I kept sensing that Judge Ito was hoping to please everyone—the prosecution, the defense, the jury, the media, the cameras, and the general public. I couldn't help feeling compassion for the ordeal. Few judges have been subjected to as much scrutiny of their personal lives. And he knew from the outset that there would be bitter opposition to whatever decision the jury might reach. While every judge must realize that each case has ramifications for the individuals involved, it must be a very heavy burden to be responsible for a trial that seemed destined to create such an enormous backlash.

Chapter 14

WAITING FOR THE VERDICT

LOS ANGELES, CALIFORNIA
SEPTEMBER–OCTOBER 1995

I don't believe there are any coincidences in
life—everything happens for a reason. Lately it
seems to me that each day brings new awareness.
I was insulted when Johnnie Cochran, in his
closing argument, cried out to the brethren of the
jury, quoting Scriptures in one breath and
referring to Mark Fuhrman and Detective Phil
Vannatter as devils in the other. What was most
outrageous, however, was that Cochran actually
had the audacity to compare Mark Fuhrman to
Adolf Hitler. He went so far as to ask the jury to
send a message with their verdict of not guilty
because racism was involved. With members of
the Nation of Islam waiting outside to protect him

and the streets surrounding the courtroom
crowded with Cochran supporters, I could not
help but question if this was a power move by
Johnnie Cochran.

The trial no longer had anything to do with
O.J. Simpson. O.J. was simply a vehicle that
Cochran was intentionally using. I kept asking
myself what Cochran was trying to accomplish.
Had he intended to stir up civil unrest? Was he
intentionally trying to incite riots? Or was it
possible that he didn't think of the consequences
of his actions? I think not! He knew exactly what
he was doing. He was drawing on the race card to
free a guilty man and, more importantly, gain
political control. While legal analysts did raise the
issue of the absurdity of the comparison between
Hitler and Fuhrman, no one ever seemed to
question Cochran's motives.

As the end of the trial drew near, the media
started asking for more interviews, and I agreed to
do some. The first was "Rivera Live," and it was a
revelation of sorts. It was no longer a matter of
explaining yet again why I had written *Private
Diary* and then fighting for an opportunity to talk
about domestic violence. Instead, I was praised for
having had the courage to tell the truth and to
give what has been referred to as a "blueprint for

the prosecution." My interest in domestic violence has been respected and I have been able to send my message loud and clear.

Geraldo was gracious and complimentary and he apologized for having permitted untruths about me to be broadcast in the past. He gave me an opportunity to answer questions thoroughly and to put my thoughts into context. However, a few weeks later I appeared with Candace Garvey and *National Enquirer* columnist Mike Walker on another "Geraldo" show and that was far more difficult—not because Geraldo had changed, but because the audience was composed largely, it seemed, of O.J. supporters. The defense team's increasing emphasis on the racial issue had had the desired effect. They had been hostile from the outset, but now they were furious. Geraldo reminded his audience that he has always been a staunch advocate of minorities, especially African Americans, and that they should know he would never be a party to anything that was even remotely racist.

* * *

In trying to gather my thoughts on the racial aspects of the trial, I turned again to former prosecutor Vincent Bugliosi for his views. His first point was that there was absolutely no valid racial issue in the O.J. Simpson case. "This is clearly and simply the case of a man who happens to be black who is on trial for murdering his former wife—nothing more, nothing less."

He added that, regardless of the long-range detriment to racial relations, the defense was blatantly and cynically willing to exploit the black community to help their client.

He pointed out that "while there is no question that brutality and excessive force have been used by a small percentage of neo-Fascists in the police force, deliberate frame-ups of blacks and other minorities for robbery, burglary, murder, and so on are virtually unheard of. Yet the defense built on the negative feelings of black jurors and sought to extend them to include a Byzantine frame-up. It was most unfortunate that the prosecution failed to point out this extremely important and critical distinction to the jury."

While I can hope that the jury looked at all the evidence objectively, there is no question that Cochran's message of a racial conspiracy had a tremendous impact on the public. Not only did he turn a murder trial into a racist conspiracy, he likened a rogue detective to Adolf Hitler. There is no excuse for the Mark Fuhrmans of the world, but Fuhrman's viciousness cannot be equated with that of a man who tortured and killed millions of men, women, and children and tried to eradicate an entire race of people. It will take many years to heal the breach that Cochran created, or at the very least intensified.

I will always think of the days of the trial as the roller-coaster ride from hell. I was so anxious for Marcia Clark to be at her very best as she started her closing remarks that I felt as if my heart were trying to help hers beat. She seemed tired and at a bit of a loss during the morning, and I kept feeling that I should be there to encourage her. That, of course, was out of the question. When I called to ask her if I could, at long last, be in the courtroom as I felt I should have been all along, Clark's assistant, Patty Fairbanks, said, "Faye, the courthouse is surrounded by the Nation of Islam and the entire street is blocked off. If you could get here, which is doubtful, you might be the spark that would set off an explosive situation."

In the afternoon Clark seemed to come into her own. She quietly and methodically reviewed the evidence and I was convinced that there was no way the jury could fail to understand and agree with the points she presented. The next day Christopher Darden was equally impressive. He made a restrained but impassioned plea to the jurors, explaining why and how O.J. had committed the murders. I didn't think it was possible that the jury could fail to understand that O.J. was, as Clark had said at the outset, "110 percent guilty."

Then came the Johnnie Cochran performance. On a personal note, I was relieved to see that he no longer insisted that the murders were a drug cartel hit aimed at me. But his new theory—that a burglar was after the contents of the envelope Ron Goldman was carrying—was equally ludicrous. If so, why was the envelope still there? In retrospect, the attempted envelope heist is every bit as logical as the drug cartel hit.

Rather than use my own adjectives to describe Mr. Cochran's histrionics, I will quote an Associated Press story:

"In the style of a revival preacher, Cochran invoked history and the Bible as he wrapped up his closing arguments and urged jurors to acquit Simpson.

"He said jurors should seize the chance to change history by curbing racism and police misconduct and freeing an innocent man—whether they have to deliberate one day or 100 days. His final words to jurors: 'God bless you.'

"Clark ended the prosecution's closing argument with images of Nicole Brown Simpson's battered face and sounds of her desperate voice. As parts of two 911 Emergency calls were played, prosecutors flashed other pictures on the seven-foot-tall courtroom screen: Goldman's slashed body, Simpson's white Bronco, a bloody glove, the crime scene.

"The tape ended, and in silence, a photo of a bloody Mrs. Simpson was displayed. Her sisters covered their ears; her mother cried. Goldman's family cried. Simpson looked away. The defense lodged more than sixty objections during the prosecution's closing argument. Ito overruled nearly all of them."

I understand that people in front of television sets across the country were in tears by the end of that tape. I won't even try to describe what it did to me. But almost immediately an amazing series of events occurred. Although Marcia Clark, Chris Darden, and the tape didn't give one shred of information that hadn't already been put forth many times during the trial, it was if lightbulbs had gone on in people's heads throughout the country.

I started receiving calls from friends who told me they now understood what I had been trying to say, and radio and TV news reports carried the story as if it were being told for the first time.

I can only wonder what the jury heard. Or were they deafened by the tangled web of lies that Johnnie Cochran worked so hard to create?

* * *

As the end of the trial approached, members of the media were eagerly trying to line up interviews and anything else that might keep the public glued to their TV sets while the jury deliberated.

One of the main reasons I was willing to do these interviews at all hours of the day and night, sometimes under very trying circumstances, is that after every show I do, I always receive letters from women who tell me that I have given them new understanding and the courage to try to leave an abusive partner and get on with their lives.

I agreed to do an interview for "48 Hours," which appeared on the CBS morning news in late September, and I worked as a commentator for "Extra." I also did interviews with Larry King, Dan Rather, and the *Los Angeles Times,* and I appeared on "Leeza," a one-hour program with an audience.

Lorraine Adams of the *Washington Post* interviewed Kris Jenner, CiCi Shahian, Grant

Cramer (a friend of Kato Kaelin's), and me about our reflections on Nicole. It is one of the few articles that has focused on Nicole as a woman, mother, and friend rather than as a beauty-queen extension of O.J.

A representative of *People* magazine was at the "Extra" taping and requested an interview with me, but remembering—in fact, still smarting from—the way they attacked me the last time, I was reluctant to meet with them again. Although I have learned that certain members of the press are completely trustworthy, I still have reservations about their general approach. I realize that I can be more trusting now because they now trust me more. But that doesn't seem very fair. Until they had, as Marcia Clark might put it, 110 percent proof that what I was saying was true and accurate, I was fair game for every kind of snide remark and innuendo. On behalf of all who might someday come forward with as-yet-unproved truths, I would urge the media to consider that there is always the possibility that they may be right. Tearing people limb from limb may make for good reading, but it is an extreme form of cruelty.

Chapter 15

THE VERDICT

LOS ANGELES, CALIFORNIA
OCTOBER 3, 1995

After reading the jury's verdict of not guilty, Judge Ito's clerk, Deirdre Robertson asked, "Ladies and gentlemen of the jury, is this your verdict, say you one and say you all?" I wanted to scream, "No!" Perhaps it should not have come as such a shock to me. I had feared, but never actually expected, that the jury would believe O.J. Simpson was not guilty of murdering Nicole and Ron.

I had agreed to be on "Extra" as the verdict was announced. I knew I would be relieved that the ordeal of the trial was over, and grateful that the murderer was being brought to justice. There was little doubt in the minds of the dozens of lawyers, judges, and other authorities who talked to me about the case that the jury would bring in a guilty verdict. I knew that would not bring Nicole and Ron back, but at least their murderer would pay for his crimes.

Although I wasn't always successful, I tried to control my emotions in front of the camera. But when—after deliberating for less time than they would have spent going for a Sunday drive—the clerk announced that the jury found the defendant not guilty on all counts, I fell apart and wept. It was so difficult to believe, I felt as if I were reliving Nicole and Ron's murders all over again.

I think back to those moments immediately after the verdict was announced, and the images and sounds of the courtroom play over and over in my mind: O.J.'s smile and wave of thanks; Johnnie Cochran's hug; Robert Kardashian's display of disbelief; the sound of Kim Goldman sobbing. Then the television cameras moved to the cheering crowds lined up and down the streets outside the courthouse, and in coffee shops and schoolrooms across the country. I was astonished and couldn't help but think, *Were these cheers coming from people who believed they were watching a football game or a murder trial—a touchdown or an acquittal?* When I heard that Juror Number Six raised his hand giving the black power sign, I wondered what issue the jury deliberated on. Was it racism, corruption, or murder?

In a trial full of twists and turns that never failed to surprise its spectators, when all is said and done, I think the black community came to O.J.'s defense when O.J. had always turned his back on them. Until the trial for the murders of Ron Goldman and Nicole Brown Simpson, O.J. was a man of no color. He rarely made any contributions to the black community. Nicole had always told O.J. how he was in a unique position to help young African Americans find their true potential, yet he chose not to help. Isn't it strange that Nicole was the one person who urged O.J. to help the African-American cause when it was that very cause that would overshadow the abuse that killed her? I thought, *we have all been victimized by O.J. Simpson, and the evil that permeated Nicole's life before her murder seems to have drifted out and permeated the world.*

After all the surprises I had witnessed throughout this trial, I still could not believe the celebrations that followed. Had people forgotten that two people had been brutally murdered? Here was a case that should have been about a man accused of murdering his wife and a young man who happened to be returning a pair of glasses her mother had left at a restaurant. The accused was, as an Associated Press report put it, "a citizen of Hollywood, a rich, successful sports hero living in the colorblind glare of celebrity." It was not about race, it was about domestic violence and two incredibly cruel and vicious murders. But a clever lawyer played what has become known as "the race card" and divided Los Angeles and the entire country into black and white. It seemed that African Americans felt that it was a victory of black over white, while Caucasians felt that it was a clear miscarriage of justice.

I've since learned that the lines were not drawn as sharply as some members of the media portrayed them. There are some whites who accept that the prosecution had not made a case that stood the critical test of "beyond a reasonable doubt." At the same time many blacks and black leaders made it clear that they deplored the outcome and the attitudes of those who made it a trial about race.

A statement by Roy Innes, National Chairman of the Congress of Racial Equality, included the following words: "This is a sad day for justice in

America . . . an even sadder day for black Americans. We have revisited a discredited era in our history—when blacks were regularly victimized by white racism. We have measured ourselves by the worst in white America . . . this is a day not to rejoice but to mourn. Blacks are no longer just victims; blacks have now joined the victimizers. Black America has lost the moral high ground."

Most eloquently, he said, "O.J. Simpson is not guilty, but O.J. Simpson is not innocent."

Paul Butler, a former federal prosecutor who teaches criminal law at George Washington University in Washington, D.C., wrote, "Many of us do not doubt that O.J. Simpson bought himself that reasonable doubt with a lot of cash. . . . I think the reason the jurors did not look at O.J. when they announced their verdict was because, like me, they thought he *probably* did it. Nonetheless, like me, they also had a reasonable doubt."

The previous statements were written with the "wisdom" of hindsight—mine and others—but the day the verdict came out, after the first few agonizing moments I had no hindsight or foresight, just sadness. Then my mind went blank and I wondered if I was having a new and terrible nightmare.

After I left "Extra" that morning, I was so devastated I went home and crawled into bed. Three hours later I was awakened by a phone call reminding me that Larry King had sent a car for me and I was supposed to be on my way to do a show with him. All the way to the station, I heard Nicole's voice saying over and over, "O.J. will kill me and he'll get away with it."

When I arrived at the CNN lot, Dominick Dunne was there as well. His wisdom, kindness, and stability enabled me to hold myself together and do something other than weep through the show. Afterward, I had to go home and tell my daughter what had happened. Francesca is only eleven, but she is wise beyond her years and understood that O.J. had been on trial for the murder of her aunt Nicole. Trying to explain the not guilty verdict to her was an unforgettable ordeal. I want her to love and believe in her country, and I don't want her to grow up thinking that money can buy justice. As I tried to help her understand that our system is a good one but it doesn't always work, she kept saying, "But, Mommy, they had to know O.J. did it. Why didn't they send him to jail? That's what is supposed to happen to murderers."

While Francesca and I talked about the verdict, my mind drifted to thoughts of Nicole's children,

Sydney and Justin. As troubled as the Browns must have been by the jury's seeming disregard of their daughter's death, a part of them must have been relieved to be able to tell the children that their father wouldn't spend his life in jail. Yet no matter how they try to protect them from the details of the trial and their mother's murder, Sydney and Justin will eventually discover the truth.

Despite the dreadful defeat of justice and the judicial team, some good may have come from the trial. An article by Stephen Labaton for the *New York Times* said, "The case motivated Congress and some state legislatures to approve tougher new laws on domestic violence, and, in many jurisdictions, the number of women reporting that they have been battered by their husbands has more than doubled." If the Canadian government could be any example, abuse is not a matter between the abused and the abuser, it is regarded as a crime. The Canadians know, and Americans are beginning to realize, that most victims of domestic violence are afraid to report or testify against their abusers. That is part of the syndrome.

Under bold letters that said, FOUND GUILTY OF IGNORING BATTERED WOMEN, Mike Littwin wrote in the *Baltimore Sun*, "There were ten women on the twelve-person jury. They looked at pictures of Nicole Brown Simpson's bruised face, heard the frantic 911 calls, listened to what the prosecutors vividly called a plea from the grave and said, in effect, that none of it mattered. "Wife-beater O.J. Simpson, the jurors concluded, was not a wife killer."

Littwin also wrote, "In the jury room, nobody even argued the domestic-violence case. Of course, they didn't have the time."

Littwin continued, "As Katha Pollitt, my favorite feminist author put it, 'In this society, juries will put themselves through incredible contortions to acquit or deal very leniently with men who assault or kill the women in their lives.'

"She should have mentioned this to Marcia Clark about a year ago. According to Donald Vinson, who helped the prosecutors pick the jury, Clark was convinced that black women jurors would relate to Nicole's story. Little did she know that the jurors may be following what some refer to as the code of silence.

"Instead, the women on the jury saw it just as the men did. As for women at large, we'll never know because pollsters didn't think it important enough to know if women saw this case differently from men."

Quoting Pollitt again, Littwin wrote, "Men aren't from Mars. Women aren't from Venus. We're both from Earth, where men are the majority culture. Women are very critical of other women, and often very protective of men."

Littwin concluded: "And so wife-beater O.J. can be seen by the jury, and millions of others, as a nice guy who couldn't do such a thing. In some sectors, he is something like a hero. Nice guy O.J. wants the kids back. If he gets custody, what would that tell you? How about this: Beating and stalking your children's mother apparently doesn't preclude you from being considered a good father."

Mr. Littwin, Nicole and I thank you.

* * *

O.J. will kill me and he will get away with it. Someday I'll stop hearing Nicole's words, but I don't believe O.J. will ever find a day when he'll be able to forget what he did. He is not stupid enough to think that a not guilty verdict means he is innocent. He will have to live the rest of his life with the blood of Nicole and Ron on his hands. While I will never stop mourning Nicole, I also will never stop focusing on the positive effect that the trial has had on issues of domestic violence and justice.

Anthony T. Kronman, Dean of the Yale Law School, said, "The behavior of the lawyers in this case has brought, rightly or wrongly, the whole profession under scrutiny." Kronman's statement doesn't seem to worry Johnnie Cochran. After the verdict, he again told Larry King on national television that he was still convinced that drugs may have been involved. He said, "We believe there's a killer or killers loose in this case."

He believes? He knows! And he knows exactly who it is!

Cochran alluded to drugs and went on to try, once again, to implicate me. What he did not confide to Larry King and his intimate circle of viewers was a remark that O.J. made at his coming-out party. I have been told by several people the exact words—and gesture—he used, but I have been unable to persuade anyone to agree to having his or her name used as a source. Until now, I have scrupulously avoided using any statement that cannot be verified by one source and preferably two. But as this intimately involves me, I will repeat what was described to me. O.J. said to a circle of people around him, "There are two people I would like to kill: Denise Brown and Faye Resnick." Then he raised his hand to his throat and drew his finger across it!

Some well-intentioned but naive people assured me that I had no reason to fear O.J., but I was not assured. This is a dangerous man who likes to keep his promises. It is common knowledge that the Browns and the Goldmans, as well as myself, have received threats on our lives. It's ironic that while a murderer went free, those closest to his victims were forced to become prisoners of fear.

Of course I was frightened, but my main concern was for my daughter, Francesca, who I'm sure will never forget this traumatic time in her life. It was more than any eleven-year-old should have to confront.

It didn't take long following the delivery of the verdict for O.J.'s "dream team" to bring their animosity out of the closet. Their big game was over and, almost overnight, the players openly turned against one another. Seeking to blunt the criticism being leveled at their tactics and ethics, they leaked word that O.J. Simpson had been in command of his own defense. That was not surprising to anyone who had ever known O.J. and his need to control everyone and everything around him. However, a few days later, when it became convenient to hide behind their coattails, O.J. was suddenly their submissive client. NBC had announced that O.J. would be interviewed by Tom Brokaw and Katie Couric, and, according to a Reuters wire story, "NBC News had a clear understanding with Mr. Simpson and his lawyers that there would be no conditions attached to this interview."

It is reasonable to assume that O.J. was planning to narrate an infomercial to follow up on his statement to a *New York Times* reporter: "I am an innocent man." Then it occurred to him that even though NBC's West Coast president Don Ohlmeyer, his good buddy who had arranged the interview, would have asked Brokaw and Couric to go easy on him, once the program got started, they might have to ask him a few questions.

The next day Tom Brokaw announced, "Mr. Simpson and his lawyers decided they could not abide by the original agreement." O.J. was then quoted as saying he had canceled at the insistence of his lawyers—the same lawyers who said that O.J. had called the plays.

But more was going on. Robert Shapiro, who had been both a close personal friend and a professional advocate of F. Lee Bailey—Shapiro defended Bailey when he was arrested on DWI (driving while intoxicated) charges—announced that he would never again work with Bailey or any other members of that team.

It also came out that Shapiro, who is known as a skilled plea bargainer, had at one point been contemplating such an arrangement for O.J. Robert Kardashian was also named as having been involved in the process. I have been told that lawyers do not even begin to contemplate a plea bargain—in this case it was to be manslaughter—unless the accused is guilty as charged.

There was never any question of Shapiro's opinion of Johnnie Cochran. To clarify his disapproval of Cochran's tactics, Shapiro publicly stated that Cochran had not only played the race card, but he had also "dealt from the bottom of the deck."

Although I never expected to think a kind thought, much less say a kind word, about anyone on the so-called Dream Team, I found myself thinking that Robert Shapiro just might be a decent person who found himself inextricably tied in with some very bad people. I suspect that he will have a long-term struggle with his conscience over his participation in that case. It is unlikely that he can undo the damage he helped inflict on the judicial system, but he will certainly be more careful about the clients he agrees to represent in the future. And about the lies he will be willing to believe about people who find themselves, as I did, fighting an uphill battle for the truth.

Many of us were, from our own individual perspectives, surprised by the outcome and aftermath of the case—none, I gather, more than O.J. Simpson. After the champagne corks stopped popping, he was amazed to find that many of his former friends and associates did not consider him a conquering hero, but a person who had been unworthy of their trust and respect. He was dropped by his talent agency, International Creative Management, and failed to land a pay-per-view television special. His neighbors, both at his condominium in New York and his home in Brentwood, let it be known that he was no longer welcome among them and, the most crushing blow of all, there was a question as to whether he would be able to continue his membership at the exclusive Riviera Country Club, his favorite golfing haven (after his front lawn, of course).

One lawyer who was described as "close to the defense" said that Simpson's situation is very different from those of Woody Allen, Michael Jackson, and even Mike Tyson, three men who were accused of sex crimes. The lawyer explained that they still had talent to sell, while Simpson could only sell credibility, which he seemed to be sorely lacking.

Johnnie Cochran complained that it wasn't fair, that "this country has traditionally taken people back who have fallen from grace." He went on to compare O.J. Simpson to Richard Nixon and Spiro Agnew. He seemed to forget that even they weren't greeted as heroes within weeks of their political falls, nor did he mention that many Americans will never forgive them for violating their oaths of office. In fact, the harm O.J. inflicted on this country may actually prove even more destructive than Nixon's and Agnew's.

O.J. is still a hero to many African Americans. To some it is, quite legitimately, because of the accidental part he played in creating public awareness of the shortcomings and abuses in the American system of "justice for all." To others, it is simply because he is still a glamorous symbol of a black man who made good.

Noting that after the O.J. Simpson case, Christopher Darden of the prosecution team would probably give up practicing law, an Associated Press story on Darden said, "Asked what he would have asked if he were interviewing Simpson, Darden replied quietly, 'I have no questions for O.J. Simpson. I know all the answers.'"

We may know the answers, but what are we doing about them? I am troubled over the racial divide that has been magnified by this case. Not only do we have the tragically widening breach between blacks and whites, we also have African Americans divided over their loyalty to one of their brothers. There are those who believed he was innocent and those who knew he was guilty. And the latter group was divided between those who felt the jury's verdict was correct because the prosecution hadn't proved him guilty beyond a reasonable doubt and those who thought the verdict was correct in light of past injustices to African Americans.

There is another side to the numbers. A *U.S. News and World Report* survey taken after the verdict found that 62 percent of whites still thought O.J. Simpson was guilty and that 55 percent of blacks agreed with the jury that he was not. While I will never understand how anyone could have the slightest doubt that O.J. committed the murders, I still find it worth noting that the gulf between blacks and whites is not as wide as the racists (both black and white) would have us believe. If 62 percent of whites thought he was guilty, that means that 38 percent agreed with those who thought him innocent. And, clearly, 45 percent of blacks thought he was guilty. So while there was disagreement, there was also a large body of agreement between the perceptions of blacks and whites. We need to remember that we don't have to agree on everything to live in harmony.

Johnnie Cochran dealt another hand from his deck of race cards when he asked members of the Nation of Islam to provide protection during the closing days of the trial. As he pleaded for calm in the event of a guilty verdict, he used other phrases calculated to incite riots. During his closing statements, he made it clear that the jurors had a responsibility as African Americans to disregard the facts and send a message that blacks were not to be bound by the evidence but by loyalty to one of their own. The black power salute from a member of the jury was a tribute to Cochran's ability to inject race into every facet of the trial.

The next blow to racial harmony came in the form of the Million Man March in Washington, D.C., organized by Nation of Islam leader Louis Farrakhan. I wonder if we will ever know how much the racial slant in the O.J. Simpson trial had to do with Farrakhan's decision to plan the march. It was announced as a day of atonement, prayer, and inspiration for black men, and although it ended up being a constructive event, it gave further exposure to Farrakhan's racist views.

In his weekly radio address on Saturday, October 14, 1995, two days before the Million Man March, President Clinton said, "In recent weeks all of us have had reason to focus on two of the biggest problems facing our country. The problem of continuing racial divisions and the problem of violence in our homes, violence against women and children. I know that all of us support stronger law enforcement efforts to deal with violence against all of the mothers, all of the wives, all of the daughters in America. But the real solution to this problem starts with us. With our personal responsibility and a simple pledge that we will never, never lift a hand against a woman for as long as we live." On the day of the march, speaking at the University of Texas at Austin, President Clinton addressed the problem of racism, saying, "The rift we see before us . . . is tearing at the heart of America. . . . One million men are right to be standing up for personal responsibility, but one million men do not make right one man's message of malice and division."

It will be a long time before this country can get back on the track of healing the wounds of racism. While we hadn't come far enough or fast enough, we were going in that direction. Now it seems we are going in reverse. Saddest of all, the worst elements in white America used the O.J. Simpson case to further their vicious agendas.

On October 9, 1995, a Reuters article stated, "White supremacist groups say that they believe the verdict in the O.J. Simpson trial will prove to be a boon to fund-raising and recruitment drives. At least two organizations—the California-based White Aryan Resistance and a Jackson, Mississippi, group called the Nationalist Movement—are already trying to exploit any racial divisions that may have been inflamed by the former football star's acquittal.

"'This is a great boon to what we're doing,' Tom Metzger, the head of White Aryan Resistance, said in a telephone interview from Los Angeles. 'My phone is ringing off the hook with new people.'"

Even the gruesome murders, the unpunished murderer, and the fact that Sydney and Justin will grow up without their mother are less tragic than what this man and his case have done to us all.

Postscript

NICOLE TEACHES

A few days after the verdict was announced, the National Organization for Women and a group of shelters for battered women sponsored a candlelight march and vigil in Brentwood near Nicole's home. It was one of the saddest but most beautiful demonstrations of love for Nicole. There were about two thousand women and men, including the guards who accompanied me. Robin and Candace were there, as well as celebrities including Jane Seymour. And my wonderfully supportive friend, Susie Fields-Levine, who was once a friend of O.J.'s, turned many heads because she looks amazingly like Nicole.

I was pleased and grateful that, although some voices were raised in anger, there was no hint of violence or racial acrimony during the hours we were together. We walked through the streets of

Brentwood, our candles glowing under a full moon, and ended up in front of Nicole's home. It was as if we were mourning together and vowing to work together, not only to help battered women in memory of Nicole, but to erase racial tensions and spread harmony through understanding and mutual goals.

A few minutes into the march I heard a familiar voice from somewhere behind me saying, "Faye, please turn around." As I did, I recognized Dr. Sandra Baca, director of The Mending Place, a shelter for battered women. We had worked together and I had come to know her well and respect her enormously. Pointing toward the back of the march, she said, "Look what we have done."

We were at the top of a small hill, and looking down and back as far as I could see, the entire length of the street was aglow with the flickering lights of thousands of candles. Tears came to my eyes and I was filled with gratitude. It was a consummate gesture of love for Nicole. I knew that I had done my job and others would carry on.

Although some of my companions went to protest and to express their outrage, I truly went in peace. When members of the media seemed to be prodding me to express anger, I said, "Our cries for justice went unheard. It is time to make sure our cries for peace are heard and heeded. I no longer need to fight alone. There are now thousands of other women who have heard the message and we will work together to bring peace and harmony into the lives of men and women throughout the country and throughout the world."

The marchers were of all ages and every ethnic background. There was a unity that, contrary to the beliefs of the Johnnie Cochrans of the world, is what this country is all about. A lovely black woman who was standing next to me as I was interviewed said, "What happened to Nicole and in this trial was demeaning to me as a black American." Her little girl added, "All those people who say O.J. is a hero should be ashamed. What kind of hero would do the things he did?" And she and another little girl who happened to be white were holding hands. Why would we want to teach our children that the color of their skin or hair or eyes makes them anything other than wonderful variations of the human race?

As we approached Nicole's house on Bundy, I was thinking of the last time I had seen it. Kris Jenner and I had gone there about two weeks after the murders. Nicole had always kept the path next to her house clear of all growth, and that day it was covered with moss. I could only think it had grown so fast because it was fertilized by Nicole's blood. And the inside of the house looked as if there had been a dust storm because of the fingerprint powder the police had put everywhere.

This time it was different. As we stood together in front of the house where Nicole had lived and died, a feeling of awe seemed to descend over us. We raised our candles toward the stars and there wasn't a dry eye among us. Even the jaded TV cameramen and photojournalists were wiping their eyes. We stood in silence knowing that we were renewing our dedication to service in memory of Nicole.

I was in the black suit I had worn to Nicole's funeral and was somehow able to truly mourn in a way that had been impossible at the church and cemetery, where O.J. seemed to loom larger than Nicole. The knowledge that I was no longer alone gave me the strength and ability to come to terms with my loss. I felt I could share the grief and shed the tears that had been choking me almost every waking moment since Nicole's death.

I put my candle in one of the special glass holders that Nicole had always loved to have glowing around her. I left it burning in front of her home and walked away feeling a new sense of peace and love.

* * *

It wasn't until after Nicole's death that I faced myself and determined that there would be very little in my life until I had spent time alone to get to know the person I had lived with for thirty-eight years. Going through the loss of Nicole and the circumstances surrounding the publication of *Private Diary* had been extremely painful, and I knew I needed time and solitude if I was going to survive.

As the trial progressed, I also realized that it was imperative for me to look honestly at my past and think ahead to my future. I had written *Private Diary* and had determined that I was going to dedicate my life to helping victims of domestic violence, but I knew in order to do that I needed to understand more about the abuse in my own life before I would be able to be of service to others.

I don't know if I was predisposed to being abused because of my experiences with my stepfather, but I do know that I have struggled with abusive relationships—emotionally and in a few instances physically—throughout my life. Similar to relationships I experienced as an adult, as a small child it was difficult to understand why my stepfather felt the need to punish me by "spanking," but I do know he continued to do it until I was about thirteen. That was when I told him that if he ever hit me again, I would leave home.

Unfortunately but understandably, it has taken time to learn the lesson that is obvious to experts and others who have grown to understand the abuse syndrome: When you make it clear to an abuser that you will not tolerate the abuse, it actually may stop. If it doesn't, you leave.

Whenever I asked Nicole, "Why do you keep going back to O.J.?" she would always give me the same answer: "Because sometimes I feel that I will suffocate without him." At that time the logic behind that statement puzzled me, but as I looked at my own life and what other women have experienced, I slowly began to understand what she was saying. *Staying* in destructive abusive relationships is the disease of being a battered woman.

Throughout this past year I have come to understand that many women—rich and poor, black and white—identified with Nicole and her experiences in her marriage. Some women talked about the seemingly minor offenses such as having opinions discounted or dismissed, others relayed more serious crimes of being humiliated and controlled, and in extreme cases women talked about being physically beaten. When *Private Diary* was published and mail started coming in from all parts of the country, from people in every walk of life, I knew that Nicole represented far more than a celebrity's wife who was murdered. Her story touched the world.

As I went through the first batches of letters, I knew that the book was being read and understood. People wrote to tell me that they were grateful that I had the courage to write what I had, how proud they were of me, and that Nicole could never have asked for a better friend—that if they had a friend who would do that for them, they would consider it the greatest gift of all.

There were letters from women telling me that they'd never had a hero before, but now I was theirs. And not surprisingly there were many letters from women who were victims of domestic violence. Some of the letters were so sad that I cried as I read them. Others were courageous stories of strength. I am including a few of the letters, without revealing the writers' identities, to give an idea of how varied and sincere they were. Most of them have been condensed, but a few, marked with an asterisk, are complete.

Letter dated March 29, 1995

Dear Ms. Resnick,

I realize that receiving a letter from someone you've never met may seem a bit odd, however, I assure you that I am not some sort of raving psychotic sending a letter to some address I found in a book in some library. I simply felt compelled to write to you and express my sympathy.

After reading your book about Nicole Brown Simpson, as well as listening to several accounts of O.J.'s behavior on television, I truly believe that O.J. did commit the murders, but I do feel that he will not be convicted. He has an excellent defense team that doesn't seem to mind deceiving everyone into letting a cold-blooded murderer go free. For this reason, I fear greatly for your safety. After all, you do seem to have knowledge of more than one account of his abusiveness, and you seem to be a credible source. I pray that he does not see you as a threat and act out in retaliation.

I also wanted to take the opportunity to tell you that I admire your strength and dedication to your departed friend. I feel I have quite a lot in common with you. I will be 21 this May, and at this young age I've already experienced many of the tragedies that you have. My entire childhood, I dealt with a mentally and physically abusive father.

At age 16, already on my own, I held my best friend as she lay dying of respiratory arrest in an emergency room. At age 17, I was subjected to the cruel life that a modeling career can bring. At age 18, I finally gained the strength to leave a physically abusive "romantic" relationship. At that time as well, I began to break myself from an addiction to speed. I was also a heavy drinker and smoker. At that point in my life, I felt I needed to "clean up" and do something constructive with my life. I left my hometown, and all the pain behind me.

Letter dated August 26, 1995*

Dearest Faye,

I am reading your wonderful book once again, and I marvel at your excellent work at describing the pain your friend, Nicole Brown Simpson, suffered for so many years.

It was in January of 1966 that I finally divorced (after 3 attempts to leave) a man so much like O.J. Simpson.

I have written to you before, and your letter to me is in my scrapbook as one of my treasures.

I am the sixty-year-old retired elementary school teacher who wrote to you many months ago. You answered my letter from a hotel in Canada.

I saw you last week on "Rivera Live" and am so proud of your courage in the face of such unfair criticism. The "dream team" concern me greatly! I fear that O.J. will "walk" and all of us (abused women) will realize a terrible setback. This man is truly a monster. I truly understand the life of Nicole. I lived it!!

My husband molded me into a "showpiece" for himself while he flirted with other women four and a half years. Since my divorce in '66 he has married four other women and I've heard (by my own grapevine) that many have suffered my same abuse. "Leopards NEVER change their spots!!" I had no children from this marriage. I raised his two by a previous marriage.

The whole thing is so like Nicole's life. Constant beatings, "put-downs," all so well described in your great book.

I admire you so much. Take care. I feel if O.J. is set free you could be in great danger.

Not every letter was 100 percent favorable—but out of the thousands of letters, less than a dozen were nasty. A few people wrote things like: "Who did Nicole think she was? She was just another pretty blonde, and people were crazy to think she was some kind of goddess." They wrote that I had seemed impressed that she was such a great mother, but that I never mentioned she got all the benefits from O.J.'s life and all she did was complain about it. Essentially they were saying Nicole had everything she could possibly want, so she should have shut up about the abuse.

And then there were four letters asking how I dared to expose my best friend's secrets. Except for those few, the letters were overwhelmingly supportive.

At first I just couldn't believe it—it was incredible that so many women would write to me. I have received, literally, thousands of letters. When I started reading them, I didn't know what to expect. I had been so misunderstood by the press that I thought people probably weren't reading the book but were just getting the address and sending letters to berate or belittle me. I just hoped for the best as I sat down to read them.

As I began to go through them, it became more painfully clear than ever that Nicole was not alone. Every day I heard from more women who wrote that they were experiencing exactly what Nicole had been through, and I realized how many Nicoles there are out there.

My grief and my distress about the way the trial was proceeding and the unjust interpretations of my motives in writing the book faded in comparison to the realization that I had a purpose in life: I had to find ways to help these and many other women.

Letter dated June 3, 1995

To Dove Books:
For Faye Resnick
The reason I am writing is simply because I myself have been an abused woman for two and a half years. Ironically, the day Mrs. Simpson was found dead, June 12, 1994, I went through the worst beating of my life. It was also the day after the birthday of "Kimberly," my

*daughter. She turned 7 on the 11th. I also kept going back
to him. So many things that happened to me are identical
to what happened to Mrs. Simpson. The closet scene,
except I was naked. The statement she made of how when
O.J. was good he was good, very good. But when he was
bad, he was bad* [not a direct quote]. *How O.J. made
her tell of her ex-"Male Friends" and how he used it
against her all of the time reminded me of another
beating I received when I was sick with the chicken pox in
March of '94. I was so sick that I did not want to be
bothered. He threw up to me if he was "someone else" I'd
be bothered, and he punched me so hard he broke my
eardrum. I've also been told no one will have me if he
can't. The threats on my life, the "stalking," stealing of
house keys, which ended up with him coming out of
hiding in my bedroom with a butcher knife.*

*I also have a friend that is my "soul-mate" as Nicole
& Faye were. We know all of each other's secrets, good
and bad. We are like sisters. If it weren't for "Shirley," I
think I'd be dead now. Drugs (cocaine) and sex were my
way of escaping the pain. I finally got him put in jail,
but he received only a year.*

*I do feel trapped because I've only been here in the
_____ area for 3 years and 4 months. He was all I knew. I
did, and still do, for some sick reason, have some feelings
for him. Everyone tells me that I'm going to be another
Nicole Simpson. And it's scary that everything from the*

"molding" to the beatings and the reasons why and how he looked in the public eye was somewhat like I was actually walking through her life.

She was a beautiful woman and she had a beautiful friend. It's awful how things must happen to make the police and the public realize the seriousness of domestic violence.

My torment only lasted two and a half years. Nicole was a strong woman to deal with it for as long as she did and she's being "patted on the back" by the one that knows how hard she tried. That's the ALL MIGHTY LORD.

As I said, I only dealt with it for two and a half years, but they were the most "intense" 2 years of my life.

I hope I have the strength to get out now. I don't want to go as Nicole did, but she is 100% happier and safer where she is.

Maybe all of this is coincidental, but I received the book (by mail) June 2nd, almost Nicole's 1st year anniversary of her death, and my "near" death ordeal is just weeks away. That's why I feel I'm writing this letter.

God Bless you, Faye, for a job well done. There are very few friends such as yourself in the world. A person should consider themselves lucky to have a companion like you in their life. I have one. She is to me as you were to Nicole.

It's just that I can identify with Nicole's life with O.J. that it's an eerie feeling. My life, from the sex to the feelings for her spouse, is the same as hers. It's weird. But your story is an eye opener for myself and everyone.

Letter dated March 10, 1995

Dear Ms. Resnick,

I know that the chances of you getting this letter is very slim but I feel I must try.

Up until last night, being March 9, I thought O.J. Simpson was innocent. Last night I purchased your book. As I started reading it the knot in my stomach got tighter, there were times breathing was difficult and now the tears are streaming. You wrote my life for the past ten years. My life didn't have the glamour or the money or the wonderful getaway trips, but it had the hell, fear and confusion that Nicole had.

I too was in a bi-racial marriage. I lived with him for five years and was married to him for five. We have been divorced now for 11 months.

Over the last 10 years I have been beaten, verbally abused, manipulated and made to feel like I was nothing. My self-esteem is totally destroyed. Even as I write this letter tonight, he has my car and refuses to bring it back. A hour ago he called just to tell me that all the problems he is having is because of me. His big threat now is, "I will take our daughter away from you."

I have no faith in the police. I too called the police on many occasions, but he never went to jail. However, the night I threw my wedding rings at him and they hit him in the face, I was arrested for Domestic Violence. After I filed for the divorce, he was ordered to leave our home.

Due to the death of my grandfather, I did not force him to leave because I left town to be with my family. The day they buried my grandpa, I returned home and he was still there. I called the Police and they told me that because I did not make him leave when the court order said to there was nothing they could do.

My divorce was final April 12, 1994 and when I moved out of my home April 29th he still lived there. The Police would not make him leave.

I can truly understand the on again off again relationship Nicole had with O.J. after the divorce. I'm going through it now. I hope someday I will be strong enough to walk away for good.

I haven't dated anyone since the day I met my ex. I have no doubt that if I ever started dating he would kill me. I have decided that I will just continue to work everyday, raise my daughter and be happy with that.

P.S. Hold your head high. You have nothing to be ashamed of.

Letter dated October 24, 1994

Dear Faye,
I'm writing to say thank you for having the courage to write not only Nicole's story, but the story of thousands of battered and abused women everywhere.

When I was 17 years old I "fell in love" with a man that was 31 and, as I later found out, had beaten every woman he had ever been with. I stayed with this man for three years, during which time I suffered many black eyes, cracked ribs, etc. Finally, I had a dream in which he drowned me in the bathtub. This was the most realistic dream I have ever had and I truly believe that God or my guardian angel or someone somewhere was telling me that if I didn't get out I wouldn't survive this relationship. I was lucky, he had outstanding warrants for unpaid child support (typical loser) and I was able to have him put in jail while I escaped. I left _____ and never looked back.

Unfortunately, Nicole was not so lucky. I get so exasperated with people when they say, "Well, if it was so bad, why didn't she just leave?" To really get away from someone with O.J.'s resources would be virtually impossible. That's why you shouldn't feel guilty. Even if you had been able to persuade her to go with you when you tried, sooner or later he would have caught up with the two of you, so what good would it have been for you both to be dead? At least this way you're here to tell the world the truth.

And I do believe it's the truth. I knew he was guilty from the start. I don't know how people can doubt his guilt. Running down the highway with a disguise, passport, and a large sum of money is not the action of an innocent man—duh! The brain surgeons who say you made all this up for the money really amaze me. I'm sure it would have been much more profitable (thanks to O.J. and his thugs) to keep quiet than to risk your life by telling the truth.

Please don't let these crazy people get to you. You are a strong woman who did what she had to for her friend. You know the defense will try to discredit you by bringing up the drugs and your "fast" lifestyle. But I really believe if you just continue to tell the truth the jury and even the diehard O.J. fans will eventually have to believe you. And even if O.J. manages to lie, charm and manipulate himself out of this somehow, we know there is a higher judge he will ultimately have to answer to. That judge created the beautiful spirit that was Nicole Brown and he will not allow the taking of that spirit in such a horrible tragic way go unanswered for.

I just wanted to write to let you know you have many people who believe you and admire you. My husband has also read your book and he is as upset about this whole thing as I am. He is black and he also is a sports fan, but fortunately he is also a very compassionate and realistic man who can see the truth for what it is. We hope this doesn't turn into a black/white issue instead of what it is: a terrible malignant disease that crosses all race and class barriers and that has to be brought out and talked about instead of keeping it our "dirty little secret" to be stopped.

If there is any way I can help you, to offer support or encouragement, please let me know.

I think of Nicole every day since she died. Even though I didn't know her, I feel as if I know you both from your book. It was so candid and honest. Also, I feel a special connection because I also went through an abusive relationship.

Her children have lost the most important person in their lives and will no doubt be traumatized by this whole thing for the rest of their lives. At least they have a lot of people who really care about them and who hopefully will be able to make sure justice is done on behalf of them and their mother.

Keep the faith.

Many of the letters I received were from women who, after reading *Private Diary,* had understood that they needed to get away from their abusers. Some had gone to shelters, others had gone to live with their parents—usually their mothers—and almost all of them were having difficulties putting their lives back on track and were asking for guidance and advice.

Each letter was different, but most had a similar theme. Too many women from every walk of life, at every educational and economic level, are trapped in abusive relationships.

I guess I kind of know what Nicole was going through. I'm a 20-year-old black woman with two kids and going through the same and I have no one there for me. Nicole was blessed to have such a beautiful friend like you. I keep reading your book. It touched me and you take care and be strong. I'm always trying to never let anyone see me down.

—"Trisha," New England

I saw and felt in Nicole a kindred spirit as I too was in an abusive marriage and felt fear, guilt, shame and if only I tried harder everything would work out. After I finally left the creep, I lived in fear and hiding and still don't let him know where to physically find me. I can only imagine the terror of dealing with this with someone who had all the money, power and status such as O.J.

—"Lily," West Coast

During the period of time when I read your book, I was in an abusive relationship. Reading it gave me the strength to get out of it. Thank you so much!

—"Mary," Northwest

When I wrote *Private Diary*, statistics showed that between two and four million women were living in abusive situations. That number seemed astronomical to me at that time, but now I know that it is very low. After visiting shelters in several cities, working in one in my own community, reading as much domestic violence literature as I could, and speaking with many professionals in the field, I have learned that the numbers we know are only the tip of the iceberg. Domestic violence is far more prevalent than any report has ever documented.

According to the National Women's Health Resource Center in Washington, D.C., close to half of all incidents of domestic violence against women identified in a national crime survey were not reported to police; 92 percent of women who were physically abused by their partners did not discuss these incidents with their physicians; 57 percent did not discuss the incidents with anyone. In a study of a major metropolitan hospital emergency department, physicians failed to ask about abuse or address the woman's safety in 92 percent of the domestic violence cases. A recent national study of the 143 accredited U.S. and Canadian medical schools revealed that 53 percent of the schools do not require medical students to receive instruction about domestic violence.

No one seems certain whether the incidence of violence has actually increased or if we're just hearing more about it. It occurs to me that as more and more women join the workforce and become more and more powerful, men may feel that they are losing control and start fighting to regain it. Since most women are not as physically strong as men, if all else fails, and sometimes even if it doesn't, men may use abuse as a way to take control. There are many forms of abuse that partners use to establish their control.

One of my new friends sent me a list from Boston that explains the types of abuse very well (see Appendix A). It is important to be aware of what is and what is not abuse.

Wherever I go now, whether it's New York, San Francisco, or my own L.A. neighborhood, people who have read or heard about *Private Diary* often take me aside and tell me about their experiences of being abused. Some of these people are so successful and well known that it seems impossible that they would allow such a thing to happen to them.

There was a time when domestic violence was considered a problem that occurred primarily among the poor. We now know that it crosses all social and economic lines, and we must find a way to cope with it in our evolving society.

Letter dated May 6, 1995

Dear Faye,

I knew a few men like [O.J.] in my time and they too threatened to kill me. The last one was so rageful he even told me he could be like O.J. I got out of that relationship and he married a woman two months later that thinks she got a wonderful, thoughtful, charming, loving, honest man. He is a TV producer, so she really thought she scored big. Wait until she meets Mr. Cheat, Rage, Pig, Abuser.

I exposed him and I think more women should expose these kinds of men. They need to get help and when women just get on with their lives and don't make these abusers pay the consequences for their behavior they continue to get away with it. . . .

Thank you for your truthful book and my sympathies to you for the loss of a wonderful friend. I know she is in heaven.

P.S. I work at the House of Representatives and am watching legislation regarding battered women. If you are ever in _____ , please call. We can dine. I saw you on "Larry King" and you handled the negative reactions to your book with style and caring.

Nicole was ashamed and terribly embarrassed to have anyone know that O.J. was abusing her. Since her death, dozens of women have told me that, after learning about what happened to Nicole, they have become more willing to confront the abuse in their own lives. And they understand that by not discussing it, they are perpetuating it.

In an interview in July 1995, Attorney General Janet Reno said, "The message is clear: We can no longer turn away from violence against women and pretend it does not exist. The wait is over, and the action has begun."

Over the last year there has been great progress. Additional funding has been allocated to shelters, and many more women have found the courage to leave abusive relationships. Those are very important developments. But we have to go further than that.

In mid-1995 Secretary of Health and Human Services Donna Shalala said, "In a country where battered women shelters typically must turn away several women for each one they accept, there should be no doubt that this funding is absolutely essential."

Of course, it's crucial that we have shelters to provide a refuge for women who are abused. But we can't just house them and expect them to become wiser and stronger just because they have "escaped" from their abusers. Even after they leave, most victims will still have many emotional ties to their abusers. Some may even equate abuse with love and have subconsciously chosen an abusive mate, especially those women who were abused as children or raised in homes where there was violence. Studies tell us that 63 percent of wife batterers go on to become child batterers—and it doesn't stop there. Battered children often grow up to be abusive themselves. Abuse is often a learned behavior, and it can become a sick family tradition. Former Surgeon General C. Everett Koop said, "If you're going to break the chain, you have to break it at the child level." Staying at a shelter without getting professional help is never an answer.

The need for intensive counseling and long-term guidance cannot be emphasized enough. Professional help for women seeking to break ties with their abusers is essential at every stage of the process. Secretary Shalala also said, "Too many women with no place to stay end up returning to the very homes where they were terrorized."

Terror can escalate to the point that the victim is no longer responsible for his or her actions. Earlier this year the White House released Justice Department statistics showing that three to four million women are victims of domestic violence every year, and one-third of all American women who are killed are killed at the hands of a husband or boyfriend.

According to the National Coalition Against Domestic Violence, violence will occur at least once in two-thirds of all marriages, and 95 percent of the victims of domestic violence are women. A small number of women who are subjected to constant torment and abuse are even driven to kill their abusers. That is another reason why it is so imperative to help these women escape before it is too late. The following letter is a poignant case in point:

Letter dated September 12, 1995

Dear Faye,

I just received your letter today! I prayed every day that I would hear from you and hoped that my letter would be perceived as one focused on Justice, as you said. Thank you so much for responding; in doing so, you've responded to the cries of abused women in prisons all across the country.

Unfortunately our meeting each other is on hold for now. Thanks to the politics of this institution, I am currently being held in what they call "administrative segregation" or commonly known throughout the penal system as "THE HOLE." I have a hearing tomorrow with the Transfer Referral Board to decide whether or not I am to be shipped to the New Women's Correctional Facility in Chowchilla, California. That's another long story! The abuse doesn't stop once you get to prison. Now my abusers wear uniforms.

I'm hoping you'll be patient and maybe it will clarify for Nicole's family what she was experiencing throughout her relationship and subsequently why she died. What's even more tragic is what she would be experiencing had the tables been turned and she was the so-called "survivor."

If women knew exactly what they're up against, it might help them break away from their abuser, instead of feeling as I do, envious of where Nicole is now.

At this time I would like to tell you a little bit about myself so you can get a better picture in your mind of who I am. Contrary to popular ignorance, battered women are not all poor, black, or uneducated. We are not the "low-lifes" of society, as Nicole's death proved. I am a 40-year-old white woman. I was born and raised in Duluth, Minnesota and moved to the Sunshine State in hopes of finding a new life away from my past abusive relationships. This was in 1984. I was very happy, single, and had a successful career. I devoted 16 years of my life to the United States Air Force, ten of which I was a military police officer. With the exception of a drunk-

driving arrest in 1984, I have always walked on the right side of the law. I was only married for one and a half years and have no children. At age 36, I for the first time in my life fell in love and took that marital plunge. I avoided commitment all my life because most of my relationships were abusive. This time I thought he was "different." I was fooled again. Now it's too late.

My case does not go way back to twenty years of torture and abuse. It only took a short time. It is, although, your "typical" case of ignorance of a jury of my so-called "peers" that convicted me to a life of incarceration. It was not because I am a dope addict, thief, drive-by shooter, car-jacker, bank robber, or child killer. I am here because my instinctive need to survive took over my fear of dying. In all of our cases, the prosecution paints a very different picture of us to an unknowing jury. My military police experience was turned into a downfall for me during my trial. Because I have knowledge of the law and weapons, I "should have known better." I was equally capable of defending myself against my husband's assaults because I was given informal self-defense training 10 years ago at the Academy. Typically I was perceived as an angry, hateful murderer who used my police experience to gain advantage over my husband. Because I did not have two broken legs and [wasn't] in a coma when I was arrested, I could not have possibly been in fear of my life. In fact, because I had only minor abrasions, the prosecution's contention was that I wasn't even assaulted. Because there were no eyewitnesses to testify that he had me pinned on the couch with a gun to my throat threatening to kill me, it was said that it never happened!! His past assaults and threats were not allowed in testimony and when the judge was told he had shot at the neighborhood children for being too close to our property, he disallowed that because it was not an assault towards ME, so the jury wondered how could such a nice man be capable of doing this to his wife. Even if you have the overrated police and hospital records, they're still no guarantee you'll be believed, as this place is full of women who had such evidence. I did not report my abuse and my fears because I was ashamed and scared of what he would do if he knew I was exposing our "dirty little secret." My parents are both deceased so I had no one to turn to for support. For the sake of keeping these dirty little secrets, wait until I find out where I will be. Once I get to wherever, I'll send you the visitation form the institution requires. Whichever prison I'm sent to, there is and always will be other women like me who have horror stories to tell. Women, who much like Nicole had called the police repeatedly crying out for help, only to be ignored until the coroner had to be called.

Unfortunately, Faye, it took the death of a man I loved to open my eyes and realize I too suffered in silence until it ended tragically. Had I had this subject and its seriousness brought to my attention through some kind of educational tool, I wouldn't be here. I am truly anxious to meet with you and provide all that you need to help save the lives of our other sisters who are still trapped in this on-going cycle of violence and death. Please be patient and wait until I contact you again. I will write tomorrow after my hearing and let you know how soon I can submit the visitation form.

* * *

There are some hopeful developments. The Conrad N. Hilton Foundation funded the development of *A Model Code on Domestic and Family Violence.* The code treats domestic and family violence as a crime requiring aggressive and thorough intervention; offers procedures for comprehensive protection orders for victims; provides that the safety and well-being of children are of paramount concern when custody is an issue; and sets forth ways for states and communities to coordinate efforts to identify, intervene in, and prevent domestic and family violence.

There has also been attention paid at the federal level: On June 30, 1994, the House of Representatives adopted Resolution 473 "to raise awareness about domestic violence against women in the United States" and resolved that "it is the sense of the House of Representatives that there is a need for a national campaign to heighten awareness about domestic battery, and to end the silence that surrounds this type of violence."

When I started receiving so many letters from people who had read *Private Diary*, I became even more determined to learn about the problems of battered women and the solutions available to them. That became the focus of my efforts and my future plans.

Statistics show that shelters for battered women have been experiencing a dramatic increase in the number of people who go to them. It started after Nicole's death and picked up even more after *Private Diary* came out.

A 1992 study by the National Coalition Against Domestic Violence reported that there were nearly three times as many animal shelters in the United States as there were battered women shelters. No later study was available, but we can only hope that statistic is no longer accurate. Whatever the count, we need more shelters for victims of domestic violence.

According to the many letters I received from women across the country, it appears that many shelters have only enough funding to be just that—

a shelter. They can barely afford to provide food and shelter to women who need to get away from a man, but a roof over one's head is not enough. Shelters must also offer or arrange the counseling that will help the women they serve to grow strong, make wise choices, and act on them. And job training is also needed to enable these women to support themselves and their children, both financially and emotionally. That takes money, and it is up to all of us to make our governments— federal, state, and local—aware of the importance of adequate funding to accomplish these vital steps to freedom for millions of abused women.

About seven months ago, after feeling discouraged over the sheer number of women I was corresponding with and the little I could do to actually help them, I began to send them the twelve steps of Alcoholics Anonymous (AA) to use as a guide for implementing change in their lives. I think many women who are in abusive situations—like those who are in situations with an alcoholic—find themselves expecting and waiting for their partners to change. Many of them have difficulty accepting responsibility for themselves and their situations. I also noticed I was losing touch with some women throughout the process of trying to help them. They would leave an abuser only to return, and I thought the twelve steps might help. I was right. Soon I began hearing that this information was helping women. I began putting them in touch with one another in different cities and somehow, over time, groups known as Domestic Violence Anonymous (DVA) have evolved through domestic violence centers. The theory of group therapy, similar to what's used in AA, seems to work well because many of these women cannot afford traditional therapy. Today the steps used in DVA are different from those used in AA (see Appendix B). In Los Angeles, DVA is directed by Sandra Baca, a psychologist and director of The Mending Place. For more information about DVA, please write to:

FAYE RESNICK
DOMESTIC VIOLENCE ANONYMOUS
9899 SANTA MONICA BOULEVARD, SUITE 650
BEVERLY HILLS, CA 90212

AFTERTHOUGHT

In his book *The Private Diary of an O.J. Juror,* written with juror Michael Knox, Mike Walker noted that a comparison of O.J. Simpson and Nicole Brown Simpson with the lovers in Shakespeare's play *Othello* is almost inevitable.

There is a point I would like to make: When Othello believed that Desdemona had been with another man, he strangled her. Then, when he realized the hideousness of what he had done to the woman he loved, before committing suicide he asked that he be remembered as one who "lov'd not wisely but too well."

Each time I think of O.J.'s words at the funeral, "Girl, I loved her too much," I hear echoes of Othello. But there is one striking difference. O.J. does not seem to realize the hideousness of what he has done.

APPENDICES

APPENDIX A: TYPES OF ABUSE

Physical Abuse: Violence is a powerful means of enforcing compliance. An abuse victim may come to believe the batterer's rationalizations that the beatings are deserved.

Emotional Abuse: Insults play a major role in abuse. They tend to destroy a victim's self-confidence and self-esteem, and cause the victim to comply with the abuser's demands. The victim often can see no alternative to remaining in the relationship.

Coercion, Manipulation, and Threats: Abusers use a variety of threats to enforce their demands— direct threats of physical harm, threats to commit suicide, and threats to expose embarrassing secrets.

Intimidation: Abusers engage in acts designed to frighten their victims—making frightening gestures, smashing things, displaying weapons, and throwing objects. In public situations, abusers use intimidating looks or gestures to communicate their wishes. Intimidation reminds the victim that the abuser has the power to enforce his or her will should the victim refuse to comply.

Denial and Blame: Abusers commonly refuse to accept responsibility for their actions and seek to blame their victims for the abuse.

Jealousy: Often an abuser's behavior is blamed on jealousy, and almost any action on the victim's part is labeled as provocative (such as talking to another person or going out with other friends). The abuser displays anger and jealousy toward the victim's family and friends. Victims report having felt flattered by these displays and having viewed them as proof of affection.

Sexual Abuse: Conflicts over sex often can lead to violence. Abusers are likely to use their power to coerce compliance in sexual matters as well as in other facets of their relationships. Threats and the use of physical violence often render victims less able and willing to resist sexual abuse.

IF YOU ARE ABUSED

There are certain facts every woman should remember:

1. There is never a reason or excuse for anyone to hit you, or hurt you, or subject you to any form of cruelty.

2. No matter how bad it may be to leave, it is much better than staying.

3. If you won't do it for yourself, get out for the sake of your children.

4. You won't be better able to take care of yourself later on. LEAVE NOW!

5. If you don't have a friend or family member to take you in, there are places you can go where you'll be safe and be given an opportunity to make it on your own.

6. You need counseling. If you have no money, there are centers and other resources where you can get free counseling.

7. If you need someone to speak with and aren't ready to tell your friends and family about your situation, you can confide in a clergyman—a minister, priest, rabbi, or other religious leader—a psychologist, or even your physician.

8. Remember, it is his problem and it is not your fault. But it becomes your problem if you stick around.

9. Even if he promises to get counseling, get out until he's proven that he'll stick to it and until the counselor assures you that he is no longer dangerous to you or your children.

10. Don't wait until next time (and you can be sure there will be a next time). MOVE NOW!

APPENDIX B: DOMESTIC VIOLENCE ANONYMOUS
Faye D. Resnick, Founder

The following steps have helped many women avoid or escape from domestic violence. Follow them faithfully and you will discover that with prayer and persistence, you will find your way to living an independent and productive life.

Step One: Acknowledge that your partner is an abuser and realize that it is not your fault.

Step Two: Decide that although you have tolerated the abuse, you will no longer do so.

Step Three: Understand that you cannot achieve the change alone, but with determination and the right kinds of help, you most certainly can.

Step Four: Know that you can find support within yourself, your church, your family, your friends, and your community to help you change the situation you have decided you will no longer accept.

Step Five: Write down the names and phone numbers of the people and organizations that can give and/or help you find the support and assistance you need, and start calling them at once.

Step Six: Take immediate steps to get away from your abuser and start on a program of action and thought that will lead to a better life for you and your family.

Step Seven: Look honestly at your weaknesses and strengths, and at the ways you have contributed to the problem and enabled your partner to abuse you.

Step Eight: Make a list of what you have learned about yourself and your situation, the positive steps you must take to recover, and the negative steps you must avoid in the future.

Step Nine: Go over your list with a person you respect and trust, and each day note the actions you have taken, either positive or negative. Pray for the strength to repeat the positives and to avoid repeating the negatives.

Step Ten: Realize that not taking the steps above will be the same as admitting that you are willing to continue being abused and let your children or others you love be abused also.

Step Eleven: Know that you are not alone: There are millions of others who once lived with domestic violence and have been able to find their way out of it and go on to live satisfying and productive lives.

Step Twelve: Join a support group and spend time with others who can help you stay on the road to recovery.

Step Thirteen: Resolve that every day you will seek guidance and strength through meditation and prayer, and that you will grow stronger and wiser in your ways of coping with life.

Step Fourteen: Help others who are in the situation you have overcome to take the steps you have taken and learn the lessons you have learned so that they, too, will go on to live better lives.